HOW TO BE A WINNER

HAROLD HILL

WITH IRENE BURK HARRELL

Cartoons by John Lawing

LOGOS INTERNATIONAL
Plainfield, N.J.

The incidents recounted herein are true King's kid adventures, but some names, places, and other details have been altered to protect the privacy of persons involved.

How to Be a Winner
Copyright © 1976 by Logos International
201 Church Street, Plainfield, New Jersey 07060
All Rights Reserved
Printed in the United States of America
Library of Congress Catalog Card Number: 76-31676
International Standard Book Number: 0-88270-456-7

This book is dedicated to:

King's Kids in training everywhere
who want to go all the way with Jesus.

"For it is God working in you both to will and to do that which pleases Him."

Contents

Foreword

My friend, Harold, writes books on how to live the Christian life in the simplest and best way that I know of. He doesn't give us theories about how the life *ought* to be lived, he shows us how it *has* been lived. Even better, in all that he tells us, he gives us evidence that it *can* be lived. Best of all, he doesn't talk about unusual, unrepeatable situations that have no relevance to us, and with which we cannot identify. He talks very straightforwardly about situations which confront all of us in our daily lives.

It is this that makes Harold's books our books. I have always leapt in my spirit whenever I have heard Harold or spoken with him these past twenty years. When he speaks, he talks about God working through the situations in which he has found himself, and he speaks so authentically that I know that I am hearing true accounts of God in action.

Each incident Harold tells of starts precisely where they start in all our lives, and that is by knocking us over. What happens when circumstances play havoc with a Christian's carefully planned schedules, when he is faced with legal difficulties, or when he finds himself facing people heavily involved with the occult? First of all, he has to recognize his own inadequacy in the face of these situations, and Harold perfectly describes this, and the angry, helpless reactions that we all have in such situations. We share those first inevitable reactions, and then we move upwards with him to where the will of the Lord is made clear, and then there is the perfect outcome.

What a glorious way of living! Life is a drama. There is never a dull moment, if only we can keep seeing what is really going on. That is the main point of all of Harold's teachings, to take the unbelieving scales from off our eyes, and to find that all life in its most ordinary forms is part of the adventure of faith.

This book will surely have the best seller status of Harold's earlier book, *How to Live Like a King's Kid.* The example that Harold shows us, of believing God and praising Him in all circumstances even before we know how they are going to turn out, is one that all of us need to learn.

In all of this, Harold does not point to himself. He points to the One who is the solution to the hard problems of our lives, Jesus Himself. Because of this, *How to be a Winner* will be a blessing to all who read it with seeing eyes.

Norman Grubb

Preface

Who wants to be a winner? Everybody.

What is a winner? Someone who is always way out ahead of the pack. Someone who is admired for special achievements, outstanding accomplishments, unusual attainments, and who generally receives special attention.

What makes a winner? How do you get that way? Why isn't everybody a winner? Why can't you be a winner?

You can!

How?

Glad you asked the question. That's what this book is all about—how to win over Adversity, Worry, Poverty, Disease, Self-Condemnation, Sin, Boredom, Fear, Anxiety, Frustration, Depression, Resentments, and all the other things that happen as a result of just being a "people."

How can you know that's not a fairy tale?

Simple. Try it for yourself.

But first, your position as a King's kid must be properly established. Then, you must know your rights and privileges as a special person. Next, you can simply stand on the promises and see the results.

Does it sound too good to be true? Yes, but it's too good *not* to be true. Because that's God's perfect plan for those who belong to Him through His Son Jesus Christ.

Is there something more you have to know?

Read on.

But first, a few definitions of the things to be dealt with in becoming a winner:

FEAR—Perfect faith in failure. The attitude of losers.

DISEASE—Dis-ease, or lack of ease in any situation. Failure to fit into your surroundings in a restful manner.

BOREDOM—Stems from lack of vision. "Where there is no vision, the people perish" (Proverbs 29:18). The perishing from boredom is generally activated by alcohol, pills, or windowsills.

ANXIETY—Borrowing problems from the future. Guaranteed to create more problems.

FRUSTRATION—What happens to people who have no invisible means of support—Jesus within—or who fail to acknowledge Him in all their ways (Proverbs 3:6).

DEPRESSION—The opposite of expression, which is the showing forth of God's grace. Depression, then, is the showing forth of the devil's *dis*grace. His disgrace is read out in his mission. The devil comes to "steal, and to kill, and to destroy" (John 10:10a), while Jesus came "that they might have life, and that they might have it more abundantly" (John 10:10b). Jesus called the devil "a murderer . . a liar, and the father of lies" (John 8:44 RSV).

RESENTMENTS—Born of faith in failure. Soulish reactions against others who are better at being winners, or who show us by the mirror principle of Romans 2:1 what we are.

POVERTY—Undesirable state brought on by self-reliance for self-gratification through self-achievement.

"BAD-LUCK"—Literally, Bad Lucifer. That's what happens to pagan brats, but King's kids never have any of it. Romans 8:28 guarantees special arrangements for every occasion. Results guaranteed.

ADVERSITY—The innate ability of human nature to snatch defeat from certain victory.

SIN—"Whatsoever is not of faith" (Romans 14:23) is God's definition. People try to cover it up with situation ethics, and the attitudes, platitudes, and man-made beatitudes of do-it-yourself living.

SELF-CONDEMNATION—Often results in pity-party efforts to cover up, which only make things worse. Caused by ignorance of the rights and privileges of King's kids and by an unrealistic insistence on instant perfection.

But enough of the dismal dictionary. If God wants all King's kids to be winners, why is it so few make it? Why is it such a struggle?

Human nature! Our old nature simply rebels at the very suggestion that God's ways are better than our ways. Rebellion is standard equipment in all human beings, and that's why, in order to begin this new life-style, you must, by an act of your own will, say, "God, I am willing for You to make me willing for Your will to be my desire at all times."

"But won't I become a vegetable?" you ask.

Just be willing for God to make you a totally contented Carrot in His garden and see what happens. You have nothing to lose except your anxiety, fear, uncertainty, worry, frustration, and all the other undesirables that are the natural results of your best efforts at self management.

"You mean I must become a Milquetoast—a doormat for everyone to walk on?"

It might seem something like that to your commonsense thinking, but remember, we are trying out God's kind of wisdom for a change.

If you will just forget all your pagan-style fantasizing for about fifteen chapters and begin applying the King's Kids in Training program for the next ninety days, you will discover as I have that God's plan really works.

What is the ninety-day King's Kids in Training program?

It's so simple that you can begin right now. No waiting period.

Every morning, as soon as you awake, thank Jesus for taking over the management of your life and affairs for this twenty-four hours. Acknowledge Him as your New Manager, Motivator, and Mind-Renewer. As evidence that you are trusting the New Manager, thank Him for everything that happens, regardless of appearances, for twenty-four hours.

"Well, but how do I know that God wants all King's kids to be winners?"

Because He says so over and over throughout the *Manufacturer's Handbook*. Such verses as III John 2 where God says it is His will "that you prosper and be in health as your soul prospers" is a clearcut statement which should settle all doubts. If you're still not persuaded, try John 10:10 on for size: Jesus said, "I am come that you might have life, and have it more abundantly."

Do you have to be a loser to qualify for the abundant life of King's kid living?

Not at all. When I began my walk with Jesus twenty-two years ago, I was president of my company and highly successful in my chosen profession of engineering. I had an ample supply of this world's goods—a lovely family, fine home, shiny cars, and everything else that the world considers the marks of a winner. But down inside, that awful emptiness and frustration that comes with worldly success had gotten worse with every promotion up the success ladder.

Then I met Jesus in my forty-eighth year and decided to try His life-style as outlined in the Sermon on the Mount (Matthew 5, 6, and 7). In every area of my life, I began looking to Him for His type of outlook in every situation. My life has been progressively and amazingly different during the twenty-two years since I became *willing for Him to make me willing!*

"But I thought God helps those who help themselves," I hear someone saying.

"God HELP those King's kids who try to help themselves," is more like it.

Please remember that we are no longer looking at things from the old limited commonsense standpoint. As King's kids in training, our wisdom is from above (James 3:17). We are beginning a real adventure of life under New Management, and we can *expect* results BEYOND THE NATURAL! In Jesus, everything is supernaturally natural and naturally supernatural!

Becoming a winner, King's kid style, involves some rather drastic changes in our attitudes and ideas about life in general. Our outlook gradually changes in each situation until we see things from God's standpoint. Don't expect it all to happen overnight. Most of us have spent many years settling for second-best results through following the loser program of this world. Unlearning a carload of second-best principles and being reprogrammed to function as winners takes a little time.

Understand that we are not claiming that this world's

system doesn't work. It surely does. But the unbeneficial "fringe benefits" of such side effects as frustration, strain, pressure, fear, etc., which go with success on that level have to be tagged second-best when we are looking at a better way (Phil. 4:13).

The door into that better way, the entrance into Winner-living, is Jesus. When He comes to dwell within us, we become King's kids, having "this treasure in earthen vessels" (II Cor. 4:7), and "the life I now live in the flesh, I live by the faith of the Son of God, who loved me and gave Himself for me" (Gal. 2:20).

"But is it really that simple?" you ask.

It has to be that simple in order to be fair to everyone. If only the eggheads could understand and enter in, it would not be fair to us simple-minded folks.

What is the first step in entering into this new world of adventure in Jesus?

Willingness. Willingness to rethink our entire life-style along the lines of the *Manufacturer's Handbook*.

Let's see what God has to say about all this business of being overcomers, a term He often uses for winners.

Overcomers (Winners)

Jesus makes King's kids overcomers of all the things in the dismal dictionary. Overcomers is a good synonym for winners, and the *Manufacturer's Handbook* talks about overcomers in several places. I John 5:4-5 says that "whatsoever is born of God overcometh the world; and this is the victory that overcometh the world, even our faith. Who is he that overcometh the world, but he that believeth that Jesus is the Son of God?" In other words, there is only one way to be an overcomer, to be a winner, and that is to become a King's kid, a child of God, by receiving His Son, Jesus (John 1:12).

All sorts of wonderful promises are made to those who become overcomers in the Bible-approved way (and there is no other way that works). God gives them

"to eat of the tree of life which is in the midst of the paradise of God" (Rev. 2:7);

they shall "not be hurt by the second death" (Rev. 2:11 RSV);

they will be given to eat "of the hidden manna," and will be given "a white stone, with a new name written on the stone which no one knows except him who receives it" (Rev. 2:17 RSV);

he will be given "power over the nations" (Rev. 2:26);

he shall be "clothed in white raiment," and his name shall not be blotted out of the Book of Life but confessed before the Father and His Angels (Rev. 3:5);

he will be made a pillar in the temple of God, and God's own name will be written upon him! (Rev. 3:12);

they will be permitted to sit with Jesus on his throne! (Rev. 3:21).

Summing it up, God says "He that overcometh (the one who is a winner) shall inherit all things; and I will be his God, and he shall be my son" (Rev. 21:7).

Losers

The next verse goes on to describe those who are not winners, those who do not overcome. They include the fearful, the unbelieving, the abominable, murderers, whoremongers, sorcerers, idolaters, and liars. Instead of getting the goodies in the overcomers' list, they wind up in the lake of fire, which is the second death. That's what second best will get you if you stick with ignoring Jesus long enough. God's best, on the other hand, is something else entirely. Hallelujah that we can have whichever one we really want. Jesus said that He had overcome the world (John 16:33), and we are overcomers when we are in Him.

Super-Winners

The *Manufacturer's Handbook* says that winners are "more than conquerors, through him that loved us" (Romans 8:37). Jesus does it all for us. By contrast, the world's definition of a winner is pretty raunchy—"a conqueror who has to fight constantly to maintain and improve his position." The world's idea of a winner is someone who wins the rat-race and becomes number one rat. Who wants to enter that contest! We've got a first-best alternative in Jesus.

King's kids trade in their former wretchedness for such delicious delectables as certain victory, righteousness, peace, and joy in the Holy Ghost. Here's how: Give up.

Our Contribution

The one thing God is lacking, which only King's kids can supply, and which, for the most part, they are reluctant to give Him, is weakness. Wherever the world is strong, God's power, which comes through on the wavelength of need, has to wait for someone to become poor in spirit so He can become their strength, life, health, blessing, and wisdom.

God's Offer

In II Corinthians 12:9, Jesus is quoted as saying, "My grace is sufficient for thee, for my strength is made perfect (perfectly obvious) in weakness." And Paul, having his eyes opened by the Holy Spirit to this tremendous truth, responded, "Most gladly therefore will I rather glory in my infirmities, that the power of Christ may rest upon me." He went on to say that he was so sold on this truth that henceforth he would actually take pleasure in his "infirmities, in reproaches, in necessities, in persecutions, in distresses for Christ's sake" (II Corinthians 12:10) because it was so good to be strong with the strength of Christ instead of his own.

Life Under New Management

All this is related to the principle of stewardship which Jesus introduced in the Sermon on the Mount as the foremost law of liberty: "Blessed are the poor in spirit, for theirs is the kingdom of heaven" (Matthew 5:3). In other words, "King's kids, why can't you realize that you were created to be containers for and stewards of heaven's best? But you can't be that until you give up title-deed to all your rights to anything and place yourself—emptied of self—in a position to contain Me and all My great abundance for the needs of others to be met through your ministering Me to them."

God's Wisdom Makes Winners

When God appointed Solomon to be king over Israel, He made available to him unlimited resources. He encouraged Solomon to request whatever he desired and assured him that it would be his. Solomon asked for wisdom to be a good ruler of God's people. In asking nothing for himself, he put himself in a position of faithful stewardship so God could give him untold wealth and blessings.

In Ephesians 1, God speaks of two inheritances: ours in Jesus and His in us. The only inheritance God needs from us that we are able to supply is an empty vessel wherein He can dwell as righteousness, wisdom, sanctification, and redemption (I Corinthians 1:30).

Possessing nothing, except the one thing required of a steward—faithfulness—we can be trusted with nothing or everything, whichever God sees fit to give us. It makes no difference to the steward either way. Then, when persecution comes along, the steward can say, "Lord, look what they're doing to Your 'me' self. If that's the best You can do in this situation, it must be heaven's best, because You in me are heaven's best—and I am complete in You" (Colossians 2:10).

Why Hesitate? Pride!

If the benefits of King's kid living, winning in every circumstance, are so specifically promised in God's word and are witnessed to through the ages by those who have followed the directions in the *Manufacturer's Handbook*, why are God's people so reluctant to enter into that Promised Land? I asked God that question years ago, after I had given my life to Jesus, and His answer came in one word:

Pride!

We read about pride in I John 2:16: "The pride of life is not of the Father but is of the world."

Our rights to ourselves—"the spirit that now worketh in the children of disobedience" (Ephesians 2:2)—keep us poverty-stricken in a set of second-best filthy rags. In that circumstance, our ego pushes our pride into believing Satan's lies, the most subtle which is "You can get along without God." This same attitude got Slue Foot booted out of heaven, and it keeps us in a position to miss heaven's best blessings.

Willing To Be Willing

Many of God's people sincerely desire the submissive spirit which is essential for winner living, but they are not aware of how to check on their true state before God. They often think they are surrendered when deep underneath they are still primarily interested in their own selves. I, too, was baffled at the beginning of my Christian walk until I asked God to show me a goofproof way of checking my motivation in every instance.

The system is so simple that any King's kid can spot check himself instantly, whenever the need arises. The need will manifest itself in fear, anxiety, jealousy, worry, and other similarly icky feelings. In other words, any time dis-ease sets in, we can be sure that we have reverted back to a position of ownership instead of stewardship for God. We react only when our rights are encroached upon. Any time we find ourselves reacting, we can detect the presence of the self-centered life, and the end of the self-centered life is not victory but death.

The opposite of *reaction* is *response*. Reaction is negative, response is positive. We are free to respond only when we are so conscious of God's abundance being available to us as stewards that there is no way we can be troubled by a negative reaction. We can respond with perfect liberty to the needs of others, instead of having the attitude, "What's in it for me?"

Ownership is a drag because it demands our all in order to maintain as well as improve our position. Life was never designed to be lived out with man as "owner." Many times, when I have just about convinced myself that there is no more work to be done in me along the lines of removing ownership-itis, I have come up against a new situation which shows me that perfected sainthood is not yet mine. In case you're prone to become discouraged as I have been on many a goof-up occasion, be comforted by the fact that we find no state of perfection among the saints in the New Testament.

The *Manufacturer's Handbook* makes it clear that they had not yet arrived. But "I press toward the mark for the prize of the high calling," Paul wrote (Philippians 3:14), and we can press toward that mark, too. Hang on, King's kids, there's hope for us all because Jesus is our completeness.

Ownership Vs. Stewardship

When the Lord is really my shepherd, He makes me lie down in all those beautiful green pasture situations where abundance is mine for the asking. Because I have submitted to His authority, He leads me beside the still waters. Then comes the restoration of my soul to His ownership instead of mine where it was temporarily misplaced because of my fouled-up heredity from the first Adam.

Jesus, called the last Adam, gives me a new start, a clean record, and a new name written in glory. He says, "Give up your self rights that I may be magnified through you." Literally, we are like a magnifying glass, the focal point where God shows up in this world, whenever we are willing to be nothing in order to show forth His everything. We can watch for quick results whenever God is given charge with no strings attached.

"Whatever you bind on earth—by ownership and possessiveness—is bound in heaven," and God will not put a finger on it. "Whatever you loose on earth—of all self rights—is loosed in heaven," and God, in the fullness of time, handles it for the benefit of all (Matthew 18:18). Any time we are in charge as owners, someone loses. But when God is in charge, everyone benefits. I Thessalonians 5:16-18 clearly states how to maintain the stewardship position: "Rejoice evermore, pray without ceasing, in everything give thanks, for this is the will of God in Christ Jesus concerning you."

Proverbs 3:5-6 says it like this: "Trust in the Lord with all thine heart, and lean not unto thine own understanding. In all thy ways acknowledge him (as owner), and he will direct thy paths." Then, whatever we do, we are God's will in action.

Real Liberty

"If the Son therefore shall make you free, you shall be free indeed" (John 8:36)—free of the headaches and responsibilities of ownership and free to enter into our own inheritance in Him, the inheritance of King's kids, guaranteed winners in every situation. Hallelujah!

When all else fails—and it will—read the directions in the *Manufacturer's Handbook* and follow them to victory.

Lord Jesus, make me willing to be willing to be Your will in action—just for this day—and if I'm not entirely sincere in this request—You just go ahead and do it *anyhow*.

1
How to Be a Winner
over the
Communication Gap

Offer unto God thanksgiving; and pay thy vows unto the most High: And call upon me in the day of trouble: I will deliver thee, and thou shalt glorify me. (Psalm 50:14-15)

Several years ago, I was at a retreat at Brevard College, North Carolina, with fellow King's kid, Joe Petrie.

"I've heard you say that Jesus can do anything but fail," he said to me.

"I plead guilty to believing that," I told him.

"Do you believe He could put you in front of a foreign-language congregation and you could bring a message to them and the Lord would give them understanding of it?"

I swallowed hard, but I had already committed myself. I couldn't afford to back down.

"I don't see why not," I told him. "After all, God is a God for whom nothing is impossible."

"That's all I wanted to know," he said, with a kind of devilish chuckle. "You're going to have a chance to test it out tomorrow night."

"Tomorrow?" I didn't understand. "Are we flying to some foreign country or something?" I wasn't sure my passport was in order.

"Not exactly," he said, "but over at Mount Pisgah, not far from here, there is a camp of Mexican bean-pickers. They don't speak English, you don't speak Mexican. I've got you scheduled to talk to them tomorrow night."

He watched me for my reaction. I just stood there, exerting all my available energies to keep my knees from knocking together out loud. But I guess I didn't look worried enough to suit him.

"If the Lord doesn't make them understand you, it's going to be a bum trip," he said, rubbing it in.

I sat down and held my knees forcibly apart. My teeth wanted to make like castanets, my stomach started lurching around, and I groaned out loud. I wished I'd never heard of a preacher named Joe Petrie, a college named Brevard, or a mountain called Pisgah.

What had me and my big mouth gotten me into *this* time? I could not come up with any good answers to that question.

Dare to fail for Jesus.

The situation began immediately to improve my prayer life. I couldn't afford to stop thanking God and asking Him to please get me out of the trouble I had gotten myself into.

2

Before long, I felt a little better even though the solution was nowhere in sight.

That afternoon, I learned that a young woman in our prayer group at the retreat just happened to be a Spanish teacher from Michigan. Hallelujah! Moses had his Aaron to speak for him, I would have Isabel—or whatever her name was—to be my mouthpiece. I could tell her what to say, and she could translate it into perfect Spanish, couldn't she? I heaved a sigh of relief.

I walked over to where she was sitting and told her about her marvelous opportunity to serve the Lord, to be an answer to prayer.

"I'm sorry," she said. "But I speak only classical Castilian Spanish—"

Even *I* knew that classical Castilian Spanish is pretty far from the more informal Mexican Spanish. My heart slid back into my shoes, and I began to complain to God a little bit.

•

Born losers hang in there until they lose their white-knuckled grip and slither blisteringly lower and lower down the rope that dangles over the chasm of hopelessness.
King's kid winners say, "Lord, I give up," and Jesus swoops them to safety and wins their battles for them.

•

"Lord, there's no way I can go up there on that mountain-top and bring a comprehensible message to a bunch of Mexican bean-pickers unless You intervene sovereignly. All my human resources have failed."

I didn't sense an ounce of sympathy coming toward me.

God seems to delight in letting me get into situations where I know He's the only thing I have to go on.

Well, I resolved to get my body there, but if God didn't have anything to say to the bean-pickers, that would make two of us. I would just have to stand before them stone dumb for whatever length of time was allotted. I hoped it wouldn't be long.

"Lord, I know that I got me into this by bragging on You, but You're going to have to get me out of it. Please?"

There was still no answer.

After supper the next day, several carloads of us from the retreat drove up the mountain to attend the great fiasco where my image would be completely ruined. Hill, the talker, speechless. It was unheard of. I kept on thanking and praising God, but not because I felt like it. There was simply no alternative for me to consider. I was hanging on His promise in Psalm 50:14-15: "Offer unto God thanksgiving, and pay thy vows unto the most High. And call upon me in the day of trouble: I will deliver thee."

The would-be congregation of bean-pickers was assembled in the vicinity of a broken-down shanty. They looked freshly scrubbed for the occasion, their hair all slicked back as they sat on old boxes and crates from the field. All were looking expectantly toward the dilapidated front porch that was to serve as my speaker's platform.

We started off with a few hymns, which the Mexicans didn't seem to understand. It was getting hotter by the minute, sweat was pouring down most of us, and the Mexicans began to look as if an early bedtime would suit them far better then anything we had to offer. I almost wished they'd

4

stage a walkout and let me retreat back down the mountain to lick my wounds.

After the hymn singing fizzled out, I asked the Lord to keep my knees quiet while I read some Scripture. I don't know what I read. I might even have had my Bible upside down. But I kept on reading because I didn't know anything else to do. Eventually, I quit reading because the somber faces of my congregation made it crystal clear that I wasn't getting through.

After I had stopped reading, I just stood there and waited. The rest of the retreatants waited. The bean-pickers waited. Joe Petrie waited. And I had a strange feeling that the Lord was waiting, too.

Suddenly a little woman sitting on the end of the porch stopped waiting. She began to shake under the power of the Holy Spirit. I had seen the woman at previous retreats, and knew her name was Sybil. I remembered that she was the quiet type, never had anything to say.

Still trembling, Sybil managed to get to her feet. She shook her way over to where I was standing. Once there, she clutched my arm and turned to face the bean-pickers. Opening her mouth, she began to speak in a Spanish-sounding language I had never heard before.

Moses, here's your Aaron, the Spirit seemed to say.

At once, the Mexicans came alive and began to look interested. I praised the Lord for the victory He was snatching from certain defeat. I did my praising silently, of course, because I didn't want to interfere with what Jesus was doing before my very eyes.

Sybil preached for about twenty minutes, her message

5

getting louder and stronger with every batch of syllables.
They were incomprehensible to me, but the Mexicans were
understanding them, all right. Their big brown eyes grew
bigger, and tears streamed down some of their brown
cheeks.

"Jesu Cristo, Jesu Cristo." I recognized that name in
occasional murmurings from the crowd. Then Sybil seemed
to invite the Mexicans to turn their lives over to this Jesu
Cristo, and all over the place I saw bean-pickers lit with the
glory of God. In the Spirit, I knew that they were surrender-
ing their lives to a God who had been made real to them there
on the mountain through the words of a little woman who
never had much to say.

Because we had waited before Him and dared to trust
Him, Jesus had done it again. The impossible.

I learned later that Sybil had been born in the very part of
Mexico where the bean-pickers lived. She had preached the
Gospel to them in their own dialect. And Jesus hadn't let that
word go forth void, He had accomplished something with it.
Salvation for a bunch of Mexican bean-pickers. They had
taken the first step on the path reserved for winners. They
had turned their lives over to the King of kings and Lord of
lords, and had become King's kids.

The next day, we loaded a station wagon with watermel-
ons and went back up the mountain for a love feast so good
that it didn't matter that we couldn't talk to one another.
Everybody was too busy smiling to talk anyway. All had
glory grins a mile wide because we all had the love of Jesus in
our hearts for one another.

I had found out, one more time, how faithful God is to keep

His word. Whenever we take it literally and apply it liberally to a situation, we find God keeping His promises: "Offer unto God thanksgiving, and pay thy vows unto the most High. And call upon me in the day of trouble: I will deliver thee and thou shalt glorify me" (Psalm 50:14-15).

Pagans don't offer their thanksgiving to God. Pagans don't pay their vows unto the most High. Therefore pagans are not entitled to call upon Him in the day of trouble and be delivered. All pagans are entitled to is a pity party. And they have to pay for their own refreshments. Nobody brings them a watermelon truckload of righteousness, peace, and joy.

Maybe you became a King's kid a long time ago, but you haven't been living like one. You can reaffirm before Jesus that you believe He is the Son of God who died for your sins and rose again from the dead. You can ask Him to take over your life in a more powerful way now that you're ready to relinquish all of it to Him. Once you've done all that, you can begin to live in the benefits promised in Psalm 50:14-15 the next time you get in trouble. You can thank God, pay your vows unto Him, and expect Him to deliver you from trouble. Then you can glorify Him. That's being a winner—King's kid style.

Lord Jesus, thank You that You died for my sins. I'm sorry I've turned away from You for much of my life. I turn my life over to You again, just now, and invite You to live in me in a more powerful way than ever before. Thank You for forgiving me for all I've ever done against You. Let Your cleansing blood purify me anew, and let me walk from this day in Your Spirit.

Take over every area of my life, and make it operate according to Your perfect plan and purpose. Thank You, Jesus. Amen.

2
How to Be a Winner over Absolutely Everything

Who is he that overcometh the world, but he that believeth that Jesus is the son of God? . . . If thou shalt confess with thy mouth the Lord Jesus, and shalt believe in thine heart that God hath raised him from the dead, thou shalt be saved. (I John 5:5; Romans 10:9)

Everything in the world as we know it functions according to certain specific laws. A law doesn't cause a thing to happen—a law explains how a thing works. And whether or not you choose to go along with the law makes no difference at all in the outcome.

For instance, the law of gravity says, "If thou jumpest, thou shalt get lumps." Now, you may not like that idea. It may bug every doctrine you ever had. But if you jump off the roof, you'll get lumpy. The law of gravity is completely impervious to adverse opinions. And it is no respecter of persons. You might be skinny, fat, small, or large; you might be a kindergarten dropout or a PhD; peasant, professional, or king on a throne—the law of gravity isn't going to repeal itself for anyone.

God, who created everything, is responsible for the way things work in the natural realm. He is the author of the principles governing spiritual things, too. He has written these principles in a book so that we can learn to distinguish between what's good and what's bad and govern our lives accordingly. We've got a choice. We can choose good or evil.

In the Bible, the *Manufacturer's Handbook,* God says if you want the best results out of your trip through this life and beyond, you should get with His way of doing business. If you're satisfied with a scroungy second-best, you can go ahead and do your own thing. But if you want T-bone steaks instead of just bones, do it His way. Results are guaranteed.

The first thing to do, of course, is to get admitted to the King's kid training camp. That's not as complicated as being initiated into a fraternity or sorority, and the benefits are immeasurably greater. The *Manufacturer's Handbook* tells you all about your rights and privileges as a King's kid. They are yours to enjoy if you're the right kind of person.

There are basically two types of persons in the world— those who have been born once and those who have been born twice. Twice-born people are King's kids, entitled to the inheritance. They are also agents in the hands of their heavenly Father to tell others the good news.

"If any man be in Christ, he is a new creature," Paul wrote in II Corinthians 5:17. Not an old patched-up creature, but one brand-new, born-again, guaranteed forever. Perfect. It is the privilege of every King's kid not to start out with a revamped failure. You get a brand-new you!

It doesn't matter how big a mess you've made of your life, you trade it in for a brand-new model when you invite Jesus to take over. From then on, you're somebody special, entitled to special treatment.

Life and death are coded into two analogs, YES or NO to Jesus.

Paul continues, "Old things are passed away; behold, all things are become new. And all things are of God" (II Corinthians 5:17-18). That means that nothing that happens to you is ever accidental after you meet Jesus personally. He's in charge of everything. Before you meet Jesus, you have to settle for whatever raunchy thing comes along, and you can't even complain about the merchandise—because you shouldn't be in that miserable pagan classification to begin with. All that Jesus bought for you, first-class all the way, is yours for the asking.

King's kids are entitled to receive special treatment because they have a firsthand, living relationship with their heavenly Father who made all things and owns them still. That special relationship is available through only one dealer—Jesus. No one else can get a franchise.

"I am the way, the truth, and the life," Jesus says, "and if you want to know God as your heavenly Father, you have to approach Him through me" (John 14:6). God doesn't have any other appointment secretary.

11

If you don't happen to like that arrangement, you can forget about being a King's kid, because the power to be a child of God is given only to those who receive Jesus (John 1:12). When there is only one doorway into a relationship, if you don't like that doorway, you'll have to go without.

To get into the King's kid training camp, you have to enter in through Jesus. The world offers all kinds of other options, it's true. Many of them are very appealing, many of them look exceedingly attractive. But none of them work.

In the world of science, we have discovered that atoms wander around aimlessly. It's called randomness. We find the same thing in some people, an aimless running around here and there, without accomplishing anything. They keep trying to attach themselves to something, or trying to attach something to themselves, to find completeness. But they never make it, until they attach themselves to Jesus.

"Only in Me will you find completeness," Jesus says. "If I'm missing from your life, you can search the world over, you can try all the options, but nothing else can fill that spot in your life where I belong."

Until you latch onto Jesus, you have only a two dimensional, empty life, even at its best. You may not realize it, but it's true all the same. Whether you're an up and outer or a down and outer, whether you're from jail or Yale, it makes no difference. Without Jesus, your life is empty. It can't be anything else.

If you have never been a King's kid, are you ready to take step number one in being a winner, in entering into a full, meaningful life as a child of God with something to offer the world of empty darkness? Are you ready to meet Jesus?

You can turn to Him right now and ask Him in your own words, in your own way, to make Himself real to you. The simpler your prayer the better. And if you can't think up any words for yourself, try these:

Lord Jesus Christ, I'm sorry about the mess I've made of my life. I want to turn away from all the wrong things I've ever done, and all the wrong things I've ever been.

Please forgive me for all that. Wash away the black filthiness that's down inside me.

Thank You that You have the power to change my life, to turn me into a winner instead of a loser. Thank You that I did not choose You, but that You have chosen me, actually picked me as a part of the human race to come into a higher order of life, life everlasting, that eternal life that starts when You move in and goes on forever. Thank You, Lord, that You've gotten my attention long enough to interest me in trying it Your way.

Lord, take over the management of my life, my affairs, everything about me. Take over the decision making, because I haven't done too well on my own. Take over the parts of my life that I'm ready to surrender to You, and help me to surrender more. Thank You, Lord, for understanding how hard it is for me to give up myself.

And now, Lord Jesus, move into my heart. However You do it is Your business. Whatever that means is Your business. But make Yourself real inside me and fill my awful emptiness. Take away my uncertainty, my anxiety, my deadness, my need for alcohol and pills. Take away my terrible resentment that life is such a mess and such a drag. Just reverse everything.

13

Thank You for Your promise that whosoever shall call on the name of the Lord shall be saved. Thank You for saving me and manifesting Yourself in me. Thank You, Jesus.

And now, Lord, help Yourself to me and keep on doing it. I'm not sure I want You to, but do it anyhow. Thank You, Jesus.

I rejoice that I am now Your people, that my uncertainty is gone forever, that I am three-dimensional, born of Your Spirit. And Lord, I'm reporting for training, ready to learn whatever You want to teach me so I can be a winner—King's kid style. I ask all this in Jesus' name. Amen.

3
How to Be a Winner
over Power Failure

Tarry ye in the city of Jerusalem, until ye be endued with power from on high. . . . Ye shall receive power, after that the Holy Ghost is come upon you: and ye shall be witnesses unto me. . . . (Luke 24:49; Acts 1:8)

Do you feel like a King's kid? If you prayed the prayer at the end of the last chapter, you are a King's kid whether you feel like it or not. Feelings are fine, but they're not reliable. Feelings depend too much on the weather and whether or not your lunch agreed with your insides. From here on, you have the privilege of depending on the truth of God's word, not on your feelings. God's word says you're a new creature because you've invited Jesus to come into your life and take over. That's all there is to it.

One of the first things that a new King's kid notices is that the Bible, that black book that used to be so dull and dusty, has some really neat things in it. All of a sudden, those things that Jesus said in the Sermon on the Mount and all that God caused His servants to write in the Epistles are interesting. Not only that, but they seem to be addressed directly to you.

They are. Furthermore, you'll find that if you take literally everything written in the *Manufacturer's Handbook*, and do exactly what it says you should do, fantastic things will begin to happen in your life. It'll get so good, you'll want to run out and tell everybody.

But don't do it just yet. The disciples probably wanted to tell everybody all about the good news, too. But Jesus said they should go back to Jerusalem first and wait for the power to come upon them. *Then* they could go tell everybody.

Jesus' last words to His disciples, right before He ascended into heaven, were *not*, "Okay, boys, I've taught you all you need to know. I'm going back to My Father, now, and I want you to get busy working on the great commission, telling everybody about Me."

He didn't tell them that at all. He told them to wait for something else to happen first.

In our modern world, we're not accustomed to waiting around for anything. If it's not instant, it's too slow. But the disciples must have believed that haste makes waste, or something. At any rate, they went back to Jerusalem and waited, just as Jesus had told them to do. Maybe they were aware that their own power wouldn't be good enough to accomplish their assignment. Maybe they realized they'd need a whole new tool kit to do the job. Maybe they just thought Jesus knew best. Anyhow, they didn't say, "But Master, why do we need to wait? There's so much to be done, we ought to get going." They waited.

While they waited, they improved the time, not playing cards or watching the boob tube, but praying up a storm. According to Acts 1:14, they stayed in one accord, with all prayer and supplication. Mary, the mother of Jesus, was waiting right there along with them.

And while they waited, it happened. There was a rushing mighty wind, and tongues like fire sat on each one of them. They were all filled with the Holy Ghost and spoke with other tongues. That was the coming of the power the disciples needed to turn the world upside down. Without any more waiting.

The coming of the Holy Spirit caused so much commotion that thousands of people in the city came running to see what was going on. Some of them probably brought buckets of water to put out the fire. But the fire of the Holy Spirit was something nobody could put out. When somebody asked a question about what was happening, Peter stood up and answered him. The same Peter who had denied that he even knew Jesus just a few short weeks earlier stood up and told everybody all about Him. And what he said was so powerful that three thousand people were saved on the spot. And all because the disciples had waited for the right moment.

•

Born losers get on with it, and fall further and further behind.
King's kid winners wait around until the right time and forge ahead without obstacles.

•

From that day until this, the world has been a different place wherever King's kids have asked for and received the equipment they need to handle their part in the great commission. Without the Holy Spirit, you might just as well

17

forget about trying to live like a King's kid. You'll never make it on your own.

How can you get the fullness of the Holy Spirit in your own life? No, you don't have to call the travel agent for a ticket to Jerusalem. And you don't have to wait around for forty days, either. All you have to do is ask for it right where you are, right now.

In Luke 11:9, 11-13, Jesus tells us, ". . . Ask and it shall be given you; seek, and ye shall find; knock, and it shall be opened unto you. If a son shall ask bread of any of you that is a father, will he give him a stone? or if he ask a fish, will he for a fish give him a serpent? Or if he shall ask an egg, will he offer him a scorpion? If ye then, being evil, know how to give good gifts unto your children; how much more shall your heavenly Father give the Holy Spirit to them that ask him?"

Spiritual paupers are the
empty vessels God delights to fill.

All you have to do is ask. Once you're equipped with the fullness of the Holy Spirit, then you're ready to go and do all the things the Bible recommends for King's kid living. I Corinthians 12:8-10 tells about the gifts of the Holy Spirit you need to do the job. They're not for you to keep but to deliver to needy people. There's the gift of a word of wisdom, a word of knowledge, faith, gifts of healing, miracles, prophecy, discerning of spirits, tongues, and interpretation of tongues.

Most of the things you are supposed to do are quite different from what you've done up to now. For instance, the Bible says that King's kids are to give thanks for everything (Ephesians 5:20). Before you met Jesus, you might have been thankful for things you liked, but for things you didn't like? No way. You didn't thank anybody for them. You griped, grumbled, and groaned about them. When things got really bad, you threw an occasional pity party with plenty of martyr pills.

How about praying for those who persecute you? That's an instruction in the *Manufacturer's Handbook*, too (Matthew 5:44). Before you became a King's kid, you probably didn't dream of praying for your persecutors. You knocked their blocks off. They had it coming. And you felt good about doing it—in spite of your aching knuckles.

Lay hands on the sick? (Mark 16:18). You've gotta be kidding! Before Jesus took over, you made it a point to stay completely away from anybody with any kind of ailment. After all, it might be catching!

King's kid living is different, all right, and so are the rules for living it. You'll see how some of the unlikeliest rules work out in real life experiences in the chapters that follow. And maybe you'll be encouraged to step out in faith and begin to live the new way yourself for high adventure in Jesus.

But first, you need to get the equipment. Winners can't get along without it.

Have you received the fullness of the Holy Spirit in your own life? When Paul saw something missing in the life of the Ephesians, he asked them a similar question (Acts 19:2). They were honest with him, said they'd never even heard there was such a thing as the Holy Spirit. Paul remedied the ıack in their education in short order, laid hands on them, and Jesus baptized them in the Holy Spirit on the spot. Instant infilling. You can be filled with the Holy Spirit just as quickly.

If it's convenient, you can ask a Spirit-filled believer to lay hands on you and pray, but if you don't have a lit-up believer handy, you can do the praying for yourself. The Baptizer, who is Jesus Himself, is eager to fill you with His Spirit so you can be of the best possible use to Him. "Ask, and you'll receive," He said. It's that simple.

Lord Jesus, thank You that You have made provision for everything I need to live like a King's kid. I praise You that You do everything so perfectly. Lord Jesus, baptize me with Your Holy Spirit. I need that power, and I want to be Your witness wherever You send me.

I ask, too, Lord, that You give me the whole package deal. Send along every gift of the Holy Spirit that I'll need to do Your will perfectly on earth as You are doing it in heaven. I ask this in Jesus' name, I know this is Your will for me, and therefore I thank You right now.

I praise Your wonderful name, Lord, for Your goodness to the children of men. You have given me Your Spirit, Your power, and Your presence. Thank You that You've given me the assignment to go forth to heal the sick, to cast out devils, to function as Your people ought to function in the power of Your Holy Spirit. Thank You that You will perform what I invite You to do in Your name. Thank You that the sick will be healed, the deaf will hear, and that unbelievers will become believers praising You. Let it be so, Lord. Amen.

4

How to Be a Winner over Your Own Motor Mouth

. . . Let every man be . . . slow to speak. . . . (James 1:19)

Do you feel like a King's kid now that you're filled with the Holy Spirit? Some people do, some don't. Some people get goosebumps on their goosebumps; others feel like nothing has happened. But feelings aren't what King's kids go by. They go by the word of God. He says He'll give the Holy Spirit to those who ask Him. If you've done your part—asking—you can depend on it that He's done His part—giving.

For a lot of people, the natural tendency after they've been baptized in the Holy Spirit is to go and tell everybody all about it—starting with their pastor.

"Man, you really don't know what it's like to know Jesus," they tell him when they've backed him into a corner the first Sunday after their Holy Spirit Baptism. "Why, man, until you get what I've got, you haven't got nuthin'! Now here's how to go about knowing Jesus like I know Him."

Strange. Your pastor doesn't look interested. He looks scared, like maybe he's about to call the paddy wagon. He'd back off, but you've already got him so squinched in the corner, he can't breathe. Mercifully, the phone rings, and he escapes your clutches. The next time you meet, he seems kind of uncomfortable in your presence. Pretty soon it is obvious, even to you, that he doesn't like you any more. The next thing you know, you're not teaching a Sunday school class any longer, you've been eased out of the vestry or the board of deacons, and you might even find yourself excommunicated from your denomination.

You probably think about trying a new brand of mouthwash or underarm deodorant—but that won't help.

Someone has said that people newly filled with the Holy Spirit ought to be locked up for about six months until they cool off just a little. They're not far wrong in some cases. In other cases, six months wouldn't begin to be long enough.

People newly baptized in the Holy Spirit have a tendency to think they can straighten out the whole world in one fell swoop. They often act as if their own improvement has been a by-their-own bootstraps accomplishment instead of a miracle for which God should get the credit.

It's better to keep your mouth shut at first. Don't give any answers until people ask questions. Earn the right to be heard. People will begin to ask questions, once they see the new life in you.

●

Born losers advertise their wares in all the media—and go into bankruptcy.
King's kid winners keep their traps shut until the time is ripe to tell the news with great effect.

●

"George, I hope you'll forgive me for saying this," someone might open a conversation, "but you used to be such a down-at-the-mouth guy. Now, all of a sudden, you look happy all the time. What happened? Did you win a sweepstakes or something?" Let your glory grin get wider, and maybe show him you have only two cents in your pocket. Don't say anything else just yet. Wait until he's really hooked. If you're patient for just a little while, he'll lay himself wide open.

"George, old friend," he'll finally say, "would you mind telling me what turned you on?"

> Church membership will get you to heaven when entering a barn makes you a horse.

Then you'll have a captive audience—but not because you've backed *him* into a corner. He'll have *you* there. Then you can tell him. He won't just listen politely, he'll hang on every word. He won't miss a single syllable.

Now, he may not be ready yet for the fullness of this blessing in his own life, but you don't need to try to talk him into it. That's not your job. The Holy Spirit will take care of that when the time comes, if we keep out of His way and let Him do His own thing.

Meanwhile, your thing is to keep cooperating with the Spirit, so that you won't lose what you've got before the other guy is ready for it for himself. He'll be watching to see if this new wrinkle in you is permanent press or something that washes out with the first shower of adversity that comes your way. That's how it is. You're going to be watched by people-watchers like never before.

"Be ye therefore followers of God as dear children," the Scripture says to King's kids (Ephesians 5:1). "And walk in love as Christ also hath loved us, and hath given himself for us an offering and a sacrifice to God for a sweetsmelling savour" (Ephesians 5:2). That's not the same as copying Jesus. We can't be like Him, and so we have to ask Jesus to live Himself in and through us.

"We have this treasure in earthen vessels," another passage of Scripture tells us (II Corinthians 4:7). People could care less about the container. What they're interested in is the source of the joy juice inside that keeps spilling over.

"For ye were sometimes darkness, but now are ye light in the Lord," says Paul in Ephesians 5:8. The light that people see in our new lives is the light of Jesus in us.

Light represents a kind of energy that darkness cannot penetrate. Darkness is actually the absence of energy, and a basic law of physics is that an energy system that's up to maximum output cannot be penetrated by a lower order of energy.

24

It works that way in the spiritual realm, too. When we're living in the high gear of praising God, which is the only gear *in* the system of real King's kids, no grumbling, complaining, or backbiting can come in to mess up the system. The Light, which is Jesus, keeps out all darkness.

"Walk as children of light," Paul said (Ephesians 5:8). He didn't mean that we'd never goof. God doesn't make us goof-proof overnight, so when you stumble, don't think about resigning your membership in God's kingdom. Tell God you're sorry, let Him pick you up, brush you off, and head you in the right direction again.

"If we say that we have no sin—if we claim to make no mistakes," John wrote, "we deceive ourselves, and the truth is not in us. But if we walk in the light, as he is in the light, we have fellowship one with another, and the blood of Jesus Christ his Son cleanseth us from all sin" (I John 1:8, 7). In other words, the burden of sin which used to be our sorry lot becomes God's problem after we put our lives in His hands.

All these blessings are just a part of what is available for the enjoyment of King's kids. And if you're wise enough to keep your trap shut until someone asks you *the* question, you'll be cooperating with God in such a way that your friends and neighbors—even your preacher—will be able to receive this blessing of God's Holy Spirit. Then you can have fellowship together in a way you've never had it before. You can be one of the big happy family of King's kids. It's worth being quiet until they're ready to hear what you have to share. After you show your new life long enough, then you'll have fruitful opportunities to tell it with your lips to ears and hearts that will be wide open for blessing. Show and then tell. Don't get in reverse order.

25

In the meantime, you can begin to practice some of the special instructions in the *Manufacturer's Handbook*, applying them to problem areas in your life.

Lord Jesus, forgive me that I've been such a blabbermouth about my new life in You. I've turned off the people You could have turned on if I had waited for Your timing instead of rushing in on my own. Give me wisdom to know when to speak and when to keep silent. Make me slow to speak until the right time. And then, Lord, please make every word I say be fruitful for Your kingdom. I ask it in Jesus' name. Thank You, Lord. Amen.

5

How to Be a Winner over Broken Bones, Too Little Time, and Standstill Steel Mills

We know that all things work together for good to them that love God, to them who are the called according to his purpose. (Romans 8:28)

Lots of people might agree that God works *most* things together for good for those who love Him, but that's not what the Bible says. In it, God says that He works *all* things together for good for King's kids. *All* things has to include spilled milk, flat tires, earthquakes, pains in the neck, *and* broken legs. I found out about broken leg benefits for myself just a few years ago.

God had directed me to finish writing my first book, *How to Live Like a King's Kid.* Instead of obeying, however, I churned out an unholy number of excuses. This was my best one:

"But Lord, I'm so busy," I said. "I just really don't have the time." It was true enough. In the space of a few months, I was scheduled for six Camps Farthest Out and numerous other conferences and speaking engagements from one coast to the other.

"Lord," I continued, "my calendar is booked solid for all of 1974 and most of 1975. Now maybe in another year or so—"

Hill—

"Lord, if You could provide more time," I said finally, "I'd be delighted to finish the book."

I prayed as if I was expecting Him to make the days thirty hours long, and allow me to live without sleep—or something. But that isn't the way He handled it. Frankly, He never does things the way I think He will.

Glad you brought that up, Hill, He seemed to say. *Nothing to it. I can give you all the time you'll need.*

And He did.

The next day, I slipped on a little bit of snow in my basement. My feet flew up where my head was supposed to be, and my right foot clobbered the wall as I went down. After the blow, the wall was still standing, and my foot was lying nice and limp. Every bone in my ankle was broken— but the rest of me landed on a pile of angel feathers. If I'd landed on the concrete floor, I'd have broken something more than an ankle. But God lowered me gently. He had calculated exactly how much time I would need to finish the book.

In a nice white concrete pajama leg, I couldn't be running all over the country to conferences. But I wasn't handicapped at all at authorship.

I had to call all over the country and cancel all sorts of good

28

things that were standing in the way of God's best. Much to my surprise, the Lord ran every one of those conferences perfectly competently without my help.

I wouldn't have ordered a broken ankle, of course, but He let me have it anyhow, and He worked it for good in amazing ways.

•

Born losers stand on their own two feet and get bunions, going nowhere.
King's kid winners can break a leg and still make progress, standing on the promises of God.

•

First of all, the book got finished. It hit the best-seller list, and letters are still pouring in from all over the world from people who have read *How to Live Like a King's Kid* and been blessed by it. Many of the readers met Jesus and turned their lives over to Him as they read. Others were filled with the Holy Spirit or healed of diseases. Some said they were delivered from addictions to alcohol or nicotine. The book got into the hands of people who wouldn't have been caught dead at a CFO conference or a Full Gospel meeting, and God reached them through it and raised them to new life in Him.

Can God work broken ankles together for good? And how!

The opportunity to finish the book wasn't the only good thing that happened.

In my home the evening I landed on the angel feathers were three acquaintances who had come to see me about some business matters. They turned into real palefaces when my ankle let me down. I got a little bit pale myself.

Before the ambulance arrived, I was having to push my praises out between the pains. Although my praise-the-Lords weren't smooth flowing, I figured God could accept them as a sacrifice of praise and put them to some good use. He did.

I kept on praising, even though a few groans crept in from time to time, and the businessmen probably kind of questioned my mental condition when they heard me praising the Lord for a broken ankle instead of cursing the snow that had slid me down.

God really had their attention when my pastor, Peter Vroom, who had dropped in earlier in the evening, went into action. Kneeling down beside me, he laid his hands on my ankle and prayed.

What did he pray? I couldn't tell you, and neither could he, because we couldn't understand the words that were pouring from his lips. He was using one of the gifts of the Holy Spirit, the gift of tongues. Men can't understand prayer in tongues, the devil can't wiretap it, and nervous bystanders can't try to change your mind about what you're praying.

Whatever his prayer was, it worked. The pain went away, just like that. If my foot had turned itself around and my ankle had been made whole at the same time, I wouldn't have been surprised, but that's not how God handled it that time. My foot was still dangling when the men in white coats wheeled me into the hospital.

The kind of prayer Peter Vroom prayed over my almost detached appendage was several steps above the old prayer of unbelief we used to pray for the sick before we met Jesus as Baptizer in the Holy Spirit. It went something like this: "Lord, heal him if it be Thy will." Then we'd call the undertaker to put him on notice that he might be having a new customer soon, and we'd send our best suits to the dry cleaners so they'd be ready in case we got invited to be pallbearers. But we don't pray that prayer of unbelief any longer. We have learned to pray a new kind of prayer.

Why didn't God heal my ankle when Peter Vroom prayed? Search me. He did take the pain away, and that was my immediate concern. He mended my bones back together, too, but that took a little longer.

**Every life experience serves a
purpose in our training as King's kids.**

As a King's kid, I've learned not to ask God why. I never question His motives, because I know that everything He permits to happen in my life is rooted in His love for me. Besides, my brain could never understand all He is doing or why He is doing it. I might not even think it needs to be done. But I don't have to understand. I just have to trust Him and to praise Him. If I begin to question, Satan throws in more questions, and I end up letting my Educated Idiot Box run my life, just like it did in the bad old days before I met Jesus. When that happens, I never get anything better than second best. It's far better for me to praise God and acknowledge that His incomprehensible wisdom is superior to my squirrel head. He still knows how things work better than I do.

In submitting myself to God's training for King's kid living, I stopped asking why and started saying, "Lord, You let it happen, so it's got to be better than anything I could have dreamed up." When I praise Him and ask Him what's in it for Him, sometimes I find there's something in it for me, too, no matter how undesirable the situation looks in the natural.

Now, I would never have chosen a broken ankle as a means of getting enough time to finish my book. I just wouldn't have finished it. And God knows how I can procrastinate and push things aside, and after a while hope He's forgotten what He told me to do. But God doesn't forget things like that. He believes we mean business when we tell Him, "Lord, take over my life and let it count for You." He sticks us to our bargains.

One of the businessmen who was at my house that night called me at the hospital the next day. He had been thinking.

"I've been in the church and other religious things all my life," he said, "but I never saw pain disappear like yours did when that preacher put his hands on your leg and prayed that funny sounding prayer. I don't understand it."

"Glory!" I shouted. "I don't understand it either."

Fortunately, my exuberance didn't scare him off.

"Well," he went on, "I want to know more about your kind of God—"

After I got home from the hospital, he came for a visit, and I told him more about Jesus. Because we have God's promise that His word doesn't go forth void, but accomplishes that for which He sends it (Isaiah 55:11), I know God is working in that man's life. A broken ankle had opened the door.

Not long afterward, God privileged me to see still another fringe benefit of my broken ankle. Because I wasn't off gallivanting to faraway places, I was available to do some consulting work in connection with a malfunction in a plant of one of the giant steelmakers of the world. They had a new mill in South America that was standing idle because the equipment necessary to drive one of the vital pieces of machinery, a big rotary dryer, wasn't available and wouldn't be for another year. One of the project engineers came from Pittsburgh down to my office in Baltimore for a consultation concerning what we might be able to improvise to bridge the bottleneck.

"I use an approach to these things that may be a little foreign to your usual mode of operation," I explained to the engineer after he had told me about the problem. "I pray."

"You what?" he asked, his voice squeaking upward and his eyebrows arching toward the top of his think tank.

"I pray," I said again. "Furthermore, it's the only way I know of to get optimum results every time. Do you want optimum results—or would you rather settle for educated guesswork?"

"Well," he said, scratching his dandruff, "this thing is urgent. You've been highly recommended, and if praying is how you'll get the answer for us—"

"Then it's okay with you if we pray?"

I had to make sure it was all right with him. After all, they could hire someone else. We weren't the only consultants in the business.

"It's okay," he decided. "Only forget the 'we' business. *You* pray, but count me out. I'll just listen." He looked around nervously to make sure no one was spying on him, and then bowed his head.

"Jesus," I prayed, "we need You to solve this problem. Thank You that You're able to do everything we ask of You, and even things above all we could ask or hope for. Thank

33

You that You made everything that is, and that You know how everything is supposed to work." Then I prayed rather softly in a language I couldn't understand. I didn't want to scare the engineer away, but I had to get on the hotline to heaven, the one that is God's channel for getting supernatural information through to us without the danger of any sabotage along the way.

As I prayed in the Spirit, I got a readout by way of a word of knowledge as to exactly what was needed to improvise an adaptation of available equipment to solve the problem. The picture was so clear in my understanding that I was able to sketch it out on a piece of paper for the engineer to eyeball.

"Say!" he said. "That looks like it would do the trick exactly. I wonder why none of us had thought of that solution—"

I couldn't resist asking the question. "Had you prayed about it?"

"Well, no—" He looked kind of uncomfortable, so I didn't say anything more about it right then. I just made him a proposal and quoted a price for the work.

Our company got the contract to build the thing. There was a stipulation, written into the contract at my request, that if it didn't work, they wouldn't have to pay us. That's not the usual arrangement in the secular consulting business, but King's kids get their instructions from God, and they can count on Him not to fail.

We had the mill running in three or four weeks, and the engineer returned to Baltimore to see me. He had, as might be expected, some unanswered questions.

"The thing is perfect," he told me, "just perfect. I've had a call from the South American plant and everything is run-

34

ning without a hitch. They're headed for full production. I
want to thank you for your help. But would you mind ex-
plaining to me again just how you did it, how you knew what
to do?"

"Gladly," I told him, trying not to shout hallelujah because
he had asked the question that left him wide open to receive
my witness. "We prayed, remember?"

"Yes, come to think of it, you did. But surely that wasn't
all there was to it—just prayer?"

"That's all," I said. I was giving short answers out loud,
but in my prayer bucket—where my gizzard would be if I
had one—I was praying up a storm. I tuned in to that prayer
every once in a while, just to make sure the Spirit was
making intercession for the man in my office.

He had no choice but to believe me, and I could see that he
was getting excited. He kept banging his right fist into his
open left palm, and his forehead was wrinkled as if he was
trying to make up his mind about something.

"Man, if prayer can work like that—" he stammered ex-
citedly.

"Prayer didn't do it, exactly," I explained. "We tapped
into God's channel by praying, but it was Jesus—that's God's
first name—who did the work, by His Holy Spirit."

He was nodding his head up and down then, as if he
suddenly understood everything—or was ready to accept
what he couldn't understand. I wouldn't have had to ask him
the question, because the answer was written all over him,
but I did anyway.

"Sir, wouldn't you like to know that kind of God?"

"Would I!" he breathed. Immediately, he bowed his head
and started to pray.

"Lord Jesus," he began. I didn't even have to tell him how to pray. The Holy Spirit Himself led him in a sinner's prayer. He asked God's forgiveness for all his years of unbelief, and invited Jesus to come into his heart and take over. The engineer got thoroughly saved right there in my office. There's no way of telling how many people have come to know the living God through that man's testimony. If I hadn't broken my ankle, it might never have happened.

Today, I know by repeated experience that God works all things together for good for King's kids as long as we're praising Him. If, instead of believing the truth of His word, I had gone back to my feelings, I would really have blown it. I'd have thrown a lavish pity party for a few weeks. That might have been good for some sympathy from friends and neighbors for a while, but it couldn't have lasted forever. They'd have gotten disgusted with me eventually, and I'd have found myself addicted to martyr pills. I might even have fallen back into paganism, slurping sorry soup all by my lonesome.

When King's kids stop praising God, they look like pagans, act like pagans, and smell like pagans. Pagans have the smell of death, but King's kids have the smell of sweet incense, the praise of His saints coming up before His throne of grace like exotic perfume. The secret of King's kids' victorious living is that we carry the atmosphere of heaven with us. God dwells in the praises of His people. That's almost like having a mouthful of God—original mouth-to-mouth resuscitation. We can't get any closer to God than praise brings us, because He dwells on that wavelength.

Have you been complaining about broken ankles, spilled milk, flat tires, broken romances, traffic jams? Has it occurred to you that God has permitted these things in your life and that He means to work them together for good if you'll just trust Him and praise Him in the midst of everything? Are you ready to leave your pity party, pour out your sorry soup, and throw away your martyr pills? Are you ready to praise God and watch Him work all things together for good for you?

Lord Jesus, thank You that You made me and that You know everything about me. Thank You now for the things that have come into my life that I see no good in. Help me to trust Your word that You'll work all these things together for good because I love You. Help me to trust You instead of trusting my intellect. Thank You, Jesus, that You have all the right answers, always.

Thank You, Lord, that You have planted Your love in my heart. Forgive me now for all my complaining, all my holding things back from Your perfect management. And bless me to be more completely Your person than I've ever been before. Amen.

I could see the judge give up right then

6

How to Be a Winner over a Tough Judge and Heroin Addiction

Let everything that hath breath praise the Lord. (Psalm 150:6)

Ralph James was one of the ringleaders in the dope scene in our area. The police and the federal narcotics agents take a pretty dim view of boys who sell dope to other boys, and so they set a trap for him.

In a parking lot where the kids gathered every evening, two new guys showed up. They were obviously hippie types, strung out, and nobody guessed they were narcotics agents in disguise. When they went up to Ralph, and told him they wanted to buy some "horse," he accommodated them. It was his last heroin sale—forever. They slapped the handcuffs on him as soon as he took their money.

Being arrested for selling heroin can be rather restrictive on your activities, even when you're out of jail on bond. At the hearing, Ralph was told that his case would come up in a few months. In the meantime, the judge told him, "Don't call us, we'll call you. Better make sure you're around where we can find you when the time comes."

It must have been kind of tempting to Ralph to take off for parts unknown. He was certain to be convicted, and conviction carried with it the unpleasant consequence of not less than five years in federal prison. That's the kind of sentence the judge was accustomed to imposing. He had a reputation for being tough.

But Ralph didn't split. He showed up at one of the King's kid prayer groups in Baltimore. And as it turned out, he turned on to Jesus there and was filled with the Holy Spirit. He became a completely new creature, on a permanent high in the Lord.

His family didn't know quite what to do with the new Ralph. They had learned how to handle him on drugs, but this Jesus business was something else. They were definitely shook up, and almost wished he'd go back to his hash and pot and acid so they'd know how to cope with him. Glory grins are rather disconcerting to be around when you don't have one of your own.

As time went on, Ralph became a regular at our prayer breakfasts. Soon he learned that God wants us to praise Him for things exactly as they are. He started putting this kind of praise into practice. He praised God for the icky situation in which he found himself, praised Him even for the almost certain possibility that he'd be imprisoned for five years. You've got to be a kooky King's kid to do that, and he did it.

When the date for his trial was set, Ralph asked his pastor and me to go with him to court and pray as the proceedings went on. We said we'd be glad to accompany him, of course, and then he said, "I sure would like to have a Christian attorney to represent me."

We prayed about that, and the Lord led us to a Spirit-filled attorney right there in Baltimore. I hadn't known there was such a thing. To top it off, the attorney had a Spirit-filled wife who said she'd come along to court to pray, too.

The five of us King's kids entered the courtroom in a high gear of praise on the appointed day. Ralph's mother was with us, but she wasn't a King's kid yet. She wasn't praising anybody for anything; she was doing the typical mamma things—wringing her hands, holding her breath, and worrying her heart out.

We all sat down and heard the three cases preceding Ralph's. Each of them involved young people who had been arrested for selling "controlled substances," illegal drugs, that is. The defendants entered pleas of not guilty, but were convicted. The judge handed down sentences of ten years, seven and a half years, and twelve years. Old Judge Snow was noted for being tough on kids who sold narcotics, but he was even tougher than usual that day.

Then Ralph's case came up.

"What is your plea?" the judge asked Ralph, no hint of mercy in his voice.

"Guilty, Your Honor."

The judge looked faint.

"Guilty? Do you realize you're giving up your constitutional rights to a jury trial?" he asked, peering stonily over the top of his glasses.

"Yes, Your Honor, but I know I'm guilty, and I am prepared to accept whatever punishment you see fit to give me."

41

The attorney, his wife, Ralph's pastor, and I were sitting there praising the Lord quietly so as not to create a disturbance in the courtroom.

The judge was shook up at Ralph's honesty. He didn't encounter honesty very often from where he sat. Picking up a file about two inches thick, he began to read Ralph's record aloud, asking questions at intervals.

"Did you sell narcotics to a federal agent in disguise?"

"Yes, sir."

"Did anyone tell you that if you cast yourself on the mercy of this court that I would be lenient?"

"No, sir."

"That's good, because if anyone told you that, they'd have been wrong. I'm never lenient with criminals. You're going to get what's coming to you."

There was no doubting that he meant what he said. Our feelings plunged to shoelace level, but we kept praising God. I could tell Ralph was praising Him, too.

God had promised, *If you praise Me, I'll change things.*

We said, "Lord, You've promised to forgive all our iniquities. We seem to have a sizeable batch of them here today. If praise works, we're about to find out. If it doesn't work, we're about to find that out, too."

About that time, Ralph's attorney opened his briefcase. Instead of taking out the usual sheaf of papers and law books, he took out a Bible and laid it on the table in front of the bench.

The judge looked at him.

"What do you have to say for the defendant?" he growled.

"Just this, Your Honor," the Spirit-filled attorney began. "The boy who was arrested last November for selling hard

42

drugs to a federal agent is not the same boy who is standing before you today."

The judge cupped his hand behind his right ear.

"Would you run that by one more time, please? You mean this is a case of mistaken identification?" He wagged his head, then answered his own question. "No, that can't be—because the boy has admitted his guilt."

Ralph spoke up again before the judge could swallow his tonsils.

"What he means, Your Honor, is that since last November, I have met Jesus Christ, and I have become a completely new person in Him. All the old me has passed away."

Ralph's attorney explained further.

"Your Honor, in addition to being an attorney, I'm an ordained Baptist minister of the gospel, and what Ralph says is true. He's been born again, so he's automatically a brand-new person. The kid who sold the dope is dead, wiped out."

The attorney opened the Bible to II Corinthians 5:17, and shoved it over to the judge. "You can read it for yourself, Your Honor. The word of God confirms that the old Ralph is dead, because the new Ralph is in Christ."

I could see the judge give up right then. Even *he* knew that he couldn't handle this case on the usual basis. It had blown his mind. He'd have to change the subject. He looked at the defendant and asked him a new question.

"Are you gainfully employed?" Most of the young people in trouble in our area were sponging off parents or the welfare rolls.

"Yes, Your Honor."

"What kind of work are you doing?"

"Breaking concrete with a jackhammer."

"This kid is doing hard manual labor!" The judge was talking to himself out loud now, often a sign of the beginning of roof trouble. This case was getting to him. "Now if I suspended his sentence—"

•

Born losers plead the fifth amendment and get locked up. The jailer throws the key away.
King's kid winners tell it all to the judge and go scot-free.

•

That was so unthinkable, the judge stopped thinking out loud, but it was too late. We had heard what he was thinking, and our praises shifted into even higher gear. It was all I could do to keep from shouting, "Glory to Jesus!" right there in the courtroom.

"You'd have to agree never to go near that parking lot again," the judge said.

If Ralph hadn't been a King's kid, he'd probably have held his breath, crossed his fingers, and said a quiet, "Yes, Your Honor," and crept out. But Ralph *was* a King's kid, living in the victory that Jesus bought for him, and knowing that God had a purpose for his life. There was something else the judge needed to know, whether it hurt Ralph's chances or not.

"Your Honor," Ralph said, "a few nights ago I was down at that same parking lot and found two girls who were hooked on heroin. It was taking so much money to support their habits, they had decided to end it all. One of them had a

44

razor blade, and they were ready to use it when I just happened to come along.

"Well," he said, "it's kind of a long story, but those girls didn't commit suicide. They turned their lives over to Jesus instead, and He helped them kick their habits. Today, they're about the happiest kids in town."

Fear is faith in failure.

The judge's Adam's apple bobbed up and down a time or two before he spoke again, and his voice was no longer stern, but kind of shaky. He didn't say anything about keeping away from the parking lot or anywhere else.

"You could be a real asset to society," he said, all the gruffness gone from his manner and voice. "Case dismissed."

There was no prison sentence, not even a term of probation. That had never happened before in that courtroom, and Ralph's mother knew it. She got saved right then and there, and hugged everybody in the courtroom—except the judge. She would probably have hugged him, too, but he was awfully busy blowing his nose in a big white handkerchief that looked as if it had never been used in quite that way before.

Ralph James has graduated from Bible school and is out preaching the gospel to young people whose messed-up lives have made them ready to listen.

Just as we enter God's courts with thanksgiving and praise, we have learned that we can enter the federal courts that way, too, and snatch victory from certain defeat. When we have no other resource to rely on except praise, praise alone will be more than enough to accomplish the clearly impossible.

Praising Him is God's chief direction for King's kid living. Literally hundreds of passages in the *Manufacturer's Handbook* tell us we ought to praise God. There is no way you can live like a King's kid without it. When King's kids praise God and recognize Him as being in charge of every situation, He changes the situation before their very eyes. What looks like down-the-drain disaster can turn into an occasion for a victory celebration in the twinkling of an eye. In the world, among pagans, just the opposite occurs. Pagans can grumble and complain so effectively, they can snatch defeat from certain victory.

Are you in trouble? If you're a King's kid, you can have Jesus for your Advocate, and His Daddy for your Judge. With that combination, how can you fail? You can't beat that relationship.

If you're in trouble, don't keep on trying to bury it. Go to your Advocate and spill the beans.

"Lord, I've goofed again. How are You going to bail me out this time?"

Don't worry, my child. I've already paid your bail and the penalty as well. I've paid any price they want to put on your transgression, and I've paid it with My blood. There's nothing higher. You can go free.

Lord Jesus, I admit before You that I've made a mess of my life. There's not any way humanly possible that I can get it all untangled, no way I can ever be set free. Lord Jesus, thank You that I don't have to rely on human possibilities, but that I can rely utterly on You. Thank You that You have taken my case and paid the penalty—all of it. Keep me in such awareness of all You have done for me that I will never stop praising You. I ask it in Jesus' name. Amen.

7

How to Be a Winner
over Grounded Planes

Be ye glad and rejoice for ever in that which I create. (Isaiah 65:18)

All things were made by him; and without him was not anything made that was made. (John 1:3)

Back in 1941 when we were just getting in gear for World War II, a bottleneck developed in the aircraft industry. Planes were being built faster than they could be gotten into the air, especially in cold climates.

One day I received an emergency call from an aircraft manufacturer in Niagara Falls, New York.

"Can you develop some kind of equipment that could start airplane engines reliably under frigid weather conditions?" they asked me.

At that time, everyone depended on aircraft batteries for starting planes, even on airfields. The efficiency of a storage battery goes down rapidly with a drop in temperature, rendering the time-honored system highly unsatisfactory in cold weather. At sub-zero temperatures, planes were standing on the ground because personnel couldn't get their engines percolating. Remember how hard it was to start your flivver sometimes in shivery winters? Planes were affected in the same way.

A lot of work had been done toward developing an engine-driven ground energizer. Unfortunately, the design had proved unsuitable because aircraft engines are highly sensitive to voltage and current values. Mechanisms on the planes were being burned up by the ground unit. This, needless to say, wasn't helping matters much.

> You don't need college
> for a word of knowledge.

All the aircraft people, including the Army Air Corps, were desperate for a solution to the problem. They had to get our planes in the air or make plans to lose the war.

I agreed to work on this essential project.

"I think we can come up with an answer for you," I told them, full of confidence in my own ability.

All this happened before I knew the Lord. Looking back, I am aware—and amazed—that because I had a Christian mother who had consigned me to salvation, the hand of the Lord was in every move I made—even before I met Jesus personally. He was looking out for me. Way back then, He was already operating in my life in supernatural ways.

As I sat and thought about my assignment and all it

involved, a concept for a ground energizer that *would* work popped into my head from somewhere outside it. I had never heard of such a thing as a word of knowledge from the Lord, but I know now that that's precisely what He gave me that day.

●

Born losers think they can do it themselves and save. They make such a botch of things, they have to hire a professional to come and undo the damage.
King's kid winners let Jesus do it for them and go first class.

●

What had come to me was clearly beyond the scope of human reasoning. It had to be a word of knowledge from the Lord that showed me the approach to take to solve the problem. That I didn't know the Lord then was beside the point. He knew me.

I telephoned the aircraft folks and said, "I believe I know how to build you an energizer that will work. How about sending me a purchase order so I can get my hands on the controlled materials?"

Under wartime conditions, many things were under tight priority schedules, but there was no hitch in getting top priority for the things I needed to put together a working model.

I needed further background data for my own computations, so I asked for clearance to run some flight tests with their equipment. They readily assented, gave me everything I needed, and soon the machine was built and ready for trial. We shipped it to Niagara Falls, and I flew up later with my test instruments.

"Well, there are the airplanes," the pre-flight engineer said to me, pointing to row after row of earthbound flying machines. "Let's see you start one."

The planes had engines which had earned their reputation for being harder to start than almost any other kind. It would be an acid test.

We plugged our energizer into a plane, pushed the button, and the engine roared to life. The engineer was impressed.

"Do you think it will start two engines at one time?" he asked me.

"Well, you asked me to start only one, but let's find out what it will do. We'll never know until we try."

We ended up starting three engines at one time off one energizer. No problem.

"Hill, you're in business," the engineer said. "Go to the purchasing department and get an order for a whole fleet of these units."

"Yes, sir."

Next, he sent me to Buffalo where they ordered enough energizers for their needs, then to the west coast and up and down across the country. Within a matter of a few months, as fast as we could build those things, every airfield was equipped with the device on which I had a basic patent. As far as I know, every airfield in the world today is equipped with the ground energizer for which the Lord gave me the design direct from heaven back in 1941.

Does God answer before we call (Isaiah 65:24)? Amen.

Have you had some measure of success in your life and thought you had achieved it all by yourself without God's help? You haven't, you know. Jesus said that He could do nothing by Himself (John 5:19). Are you more able than He was?

Father, I confess that I have taken credit for the work of my hands. Forgive me for thinking that anything good could come from me. Make me constantly aware that every good and perfect gift comes from You and that I am only a channel for *Your* working. Lord, make me a cooperative channel, fitting in with all Your plans, always consciously looking to You. Thank You, Lord.

And now, Jesus, let me die more and more to self, that Your name might be glorified in every act and aspect of my whole life. In Jesus' name, Amen.

"Suddenly I was awake. I saw the door opening, a crack of light...then a man-shaped shadow blotted out part of the light."

8

How to Be a Winner over Blizzards, Burglars, and Bugaboos

Trust in the Lord with all thine heart; and lean not unto thine own understanding. In all thy ways acknowledge him, and he shall direct thy paths. (Proverbs 3:5-6)

An unexpected, unannounced blizzard set in late one Saturday afternoon while I was participating in a Faith at Work Conference at the old Statler Hotel in New York City. The whole conference was suddenly snowbound. All roads out of the city were closed.

I went to my room late Saturday night after a prolonged and juicy prayer meeting. Finding my roommate already asleep, I got ready for bed as quickly as possible. It didn't occur to me to check the lock on the door. Actually, I was probably too high on Jesus to have stooped low enough to look at the lock if I had thought of it. The next day, I recalled that the door was the kind that had to be locked from the inside with a key, but that night, I just fell into bed and went to sleep praising the Lord.

Just as suddenly, I was awake. I saw the door opening, a crack of light on the wall and floor growing steadily wider as the hallway light came into the room. Then a man-shaped shadow blotted out part of the light as someone tiptoed in.

The natural thing would have been to go into action—to grab the intruder, clobber him with a lamp or something, and sit on him until the authorities arrived. But God had other plans. I didn't move a muscle, because the Lord blacked me out completely. If I had moved, the burglar would have beaten my brains out.

How long I was unconscious, I don't know, but the next thing I was aware of was the door closing again. The strip of light narrowed into nothing as the intruder's shadow stole out of the room.

"Praise the Lord, we've been robbed," I said to myself. Utterly unconcerned, I turned over, and went immediately back to sleep.

The next morning, I awoke with the events of the night before in the front of my mind. "I believe we were robbed last night," I reminded myself. Sure enough, I found that my wallet was missing. All my money, papers, and credit cards were gone without a trace.

I shook my roommate's shoulder to share the good news with him.

"Check your belongings to see if the same thing happened to you that happened to me last night," I told him. "See if someone has kindly relieved you of all your worldly possessions."

He got up to look, all 350 pounds of him. His name was Aga Khan, and he was the biggest, blackest saint I have ever seen. Aga had been a vicious gang leader in New York before he met Jesus. Now, every inch of him shone with the glory of heaven.

The thief had pulled a double-header. Aga found that his wallet was gone, too. He and I, both being kooky King's kids, did the best thing we could do under the circumstances. We praised Jesus, hugged necks, and rejoiced in the Lord. Only our consideration for the people who might be sleeping in the room below ours kept us from leaping and dancing in the Spirit. Then we knelt beside the bed and asked Jesus to forgive the thief just as He had forgiven the one on the cross beside Him.

Perfect peace set in. We knew we didn't have to worry about money. We didn't have any money to worry about. Hallelujah!

•

Born losers lock their door, stay on the lookout, and turn into nervous wrecks protecting their property.
King's kid winners resist not evil. They can get their beauty sleep while the Lord takes care of everything for them.

•

Just as we finished our prayer, the phone rang. The call was from another member of the Faith at Work team staying at the same hotel.

"My husband and I were just praying," she said, "and it came to us that maybe you had need of something—"

We hallelujahed, told her what had happened, and got

57

ourselves invited to breakfast. This was handy, since we were without funds. King's kids always take care of other King's kids who have no visible means of support.

We had planned to leave for home on Sunday afternoon, but the blizzard decreed that everybody in New York would have to stay put until Monday morning at which time some of the roads would be cleared. Having my travel plans changed wasn't any particular burden to me, because I had learned that my life was not my own and that God's plans were always far more exciting than anything I could dream up. I wondered what He had in store for me this time. It was beginning to shape up as a rather interesting weekend. A blizzard and a burglary—what next, Lord?

Sometime Sunday afternoon somebody announced that Marble Collegiate Church, which is within easy walking distance of the Statler, was having a fellowship supper that night for young married couples. Having been relieved of all my green stuff, I was willing to walk in any direction for free groceries.

About a dozen of us from the conference bundled up and snowshoed our way to the church at supper time. We didn't all look like young married couples, but they welcomed us to the table anyway. After a hearty meal, I headed for the checkroom to get my overcoat, intending to walk back to my hotel for another prayer meeting. But before I could get my arms in the sleeves, the Lord seemed to say to me, *Hang your coat back up, Hill. I want you to stick around. You have an assignment here.*

"But Lord," I argued, just as if He didn't have all the pertinent facts at His command, "I don't need to stay to hear the reports of the FAW teams. I've been part of them the whole weekend, remember? It doesn't make sense for me to sit here and listen when I could be fellowshiping with the brethren back at the Statler—"

God let me argue all I wanted to, but He refused to argue back. Finally I realized that He wasn't being persuaded to change His mind. I put my coat back on a hanger and went into the meeting room and sat down. I had learned before that it never profits me to try to make sense out of what the Lord tells me to do. He always has His reasons. He doesn't always bother to tell me what they are.

The chairman opened the meeting with a prayer and announced that the first thing on the agenda was a song service. The song leader came forward, opened a hymnal as if he was about to lead us in singing, and then stopped abruptly. His whole expression changed; the fakey smile of welcome melted off his face and gave way to a sick, gray look.

"I have something to say to the group here tonight," he announced. "I know it won't be favorably received. In fact, I'm certain that you'll reject me one hundred per cent."

After a lead-in like that, everybody had their antennae unrolled high into the air. Nobody missed what he said next.

"This is the hardest thing I've ever done in all my life," he said, "and I don't know why I'm doing it now. But I am compelled to tell you that—" He closed the hymnal, swallowed hard, and forced the words out "—I am a homosexual."

A horrified shudder went through the auditorium. People seemed to shrink back inside their clothes.

Now do you know why you're here? the Lord seemed to be asking me. I noticed that I was nodding my head in affirmation. In the midst of the dead silence, I raised my hand. The chairman recognized me, and I stood up.

"I happen to know something about what this man is

talking about," I said, "because I, too, have a dread disease. Mine is alcoholism. When my disease is active, I'm repulsive to be around, but my disease has been arrested by the grace of God. That same grace is available for everyone, and I have a strong urge to pray for this man."

Nobody leaped up to join me, so I turned to the man with the problem and asked if he would let me pray for him. He nodded his eager willingness, and we walked together to a little counseling office just off the meeting room. All eyes followed us there, but no one else moved.

No amount of willpower will
return a pickle to cucumberhood.
But God-power can do it
in the twinkling of an eye.

The erstwhile song leader sat down in a chair and closed his eyes. I laid hands on him and prayed in the Spirit for a few moments. That's all it took. He gave a sort of shiver, shuddered for a second, and then looked up with new eyes, eyes that held no trace of the haunted ugliness I had seen there in the beginning.

"Praise God!" He almost shouted and I almost shouted along with him. "This is the first time I've been free in nearly eighteen years! Praise God!"

As I had prayed in the Spirit, a prayer the devil couldn't wiretap, a homosexual demon had gone out of the man. He had felt it go. That was worth shouting about.

Right then, I knew why there had been a blizzard, why I

had been robbed, and why God had invited me to stick around after supper at Marble Collegiate. One of His lost ones needed deliverance, and that was my assignment. Where King's kids are sold out to the King, letting Him direct their paths, anything can happen. And it usually does.

Have you been acknowledging the sovereignty of God in everything that affects your life—blizzards, burglaries, boo-boos, and all? Or have you been complaining about more things than you have been praising God for? Have you been fitting into His plans for you even when they didn't match your own? Or have you insisted on doing your own thing and so have missed God's best for you? If you are ready to change, tell Him so. He'll take you up on it.

Lord Jesus, I confess that I've been following the ways of the world in lots of things. I've been complaining when someone violates my rights. I've been grumbling when weather or anything else upsets my carefully laid plans.

Lord, cleanse me of all this. Take my life and run it in a way that is pleasing to You. Don't even bother to consult me about it. Just do it. Set me on the path You have prepared for me. Use me, Lord, to reach someone for You. I ask it in Jesus' wonderful name. Amen.

9

How to Be a Winner over Buried Guilt, Dry Bones, and Corpuscle Shortage

Confess your faults one to another, and pray one for another, that ye may be healed. (James 5:16)

One balmy spring day, King David was up on the rooftop watching color television, a live performance emanating from a neighboring garden just below him. The actress was Bathsheba, and her costume left nothing to the imagination. It was absolutely gorgeous. (Live or rerun, the boob tube will get you in trouble.)

David must have thought he was watching a commercial, because when he saw Bathsheba, he panted, "I'll take one of those." He sent one of his servants to pick up the merchandise, and Bathsheba was delivered right to the door of his bedroom.

He saw, she came, sin conquered. It'll do it every time.

The first installment of sin was so pleasurable, David decided he'd like to keep the lovely lady around on a long-term basis. Trouble was, she had a husband already, a soldier in David's army. That was easy enough to remedy. David simply had him sent to the front lines where he was killed off. After all, a king has the right to order his troops around.

> Temptation is God's microscope
> for revealing hidden affinities.

Can't you hear David rationalizing to himself?

"I'm the king. I'm the head man in this outfit. I can't be guilty of stealing, because everything in my kingdom belongs to me. Even when I take another man's wife, it's legal. And when I sent Bathsheba's husband to the front lines, why, that was kosher, too, strictly on the up and up. What's a king for if he can't run things? After all, somebody has to serve on the front lines. I've served there myself. Why, when that giant Goliath was scaring the whole nation to death, I took him on single-handed—"

But King David's body didn't know that he was such a good guy. Down deep, below all the rationalizing, David knew he had done wrong. And the buried guilt began to read out in symptoms in his body.

Buried guilt, guilt that is not acknowledged before men or before God, is called iniquity. Iniquity rots your insides out. Very often it reads out in foul diseases like cancer and leukemia. God gets blamed for causing these diseases, but sometimes they're our own fault. Here's how it works:

The red cells of your blood system haul food around the body, like tiny grocery wagons that collect the garbage as they go. Their work is so heavy, carrying a load of goodies or garbage all the time, that they wear out every thirty to forty days. You would, too, if you worked twenty-four hours a day, seven days, a week, fifty-two weeks a year. But fortunately, there are always enough of the little tnings to go around. God has arranged for the red cells to be replenished continually by a manufacturing plant right in your body.

●

Born losers try to cover up their sins. They die of dread diseases.
King's kid winners confess everything to Jesus and stay healthy.

●

When the worn-out red cells are dumped overboard, you get a brand-new labor force, ready to go to work. These new red cells are manufactured in the bone marrow. The factory is so important that God has armor-plated it by placing it inside the biggest bones of your body for the utmost protection. If anything happens to that factory, you get in bad shape fast. Soon there aren't enough red cells to do the job. Leukemia, anemia, and many kinds of cancer begin to manifest themselves when there's an imbalance in your blood.

Let's say you recognize that you are guilty about something, but instead of confessing it, you keep it a secret. You bury your guilt and try to forget all about it. But it won't work. Buried guilt will make you so miserable, eventually you'll have to make an appointment with a pagan head-shrinker. He'll listen to your troubles, nod his head, and haul out his three-point program: know yourself, accept yourself, express yourself. The program boils down to, "Do your own thing, don't feel guilty about it, and you'll get in good shape."

You try it, maybe, but it doesn't work for you. Instead of getting better, you get worse. Trying to know yourself, looking deep inside, doesn't free you from mental anguish, it makes you sick to your stomach. Know yourself? Ugh!

Tell your pagan psychiatrist how you reacted toward your self-examination—you voted for suicide—and he'll encourage you to take a further step toward "healing."

"Go out and act like yourself and you'll feel better," he tells you.

You do it and wind up in jail. Your misery has been multiplied.

By nature, all of us are real slobs. There's not enough human righteousness in the whole world to whitewash even one of us. Not enough Brownie points, either.

"Blessed is he whose transgression is forgiven, whose sin is covered," David wrote (Psalm 32:1). And the only covering for sin that God recognizes is the red blood of Jesus. If you try to cover sin with your own self-righteousness, you're really asking for trouble. All our righteousness is as filthy rags in God's sight. Filthy rags are the worst possible covering for a sore. They make excellent breeding grounds for maggots. Under the maggoty bandages of good-guy righteousness, gangrene gets going at a galloping rate.

King David, the man after God's own heart, began to get in such bad shape from his buried iniquity that he had to let God deal with it—or die. In the 32nd Psalm, he tells how it was with him:

"When I kept silence," David said, "when I refused to acknowledge that I was at fault, my bones waxed old." Old bones have marrow that is all dried up. Buried guilt goes right through the armor plate of bone, right down into the marrow. And the consequences? Today we would say that David had all the symptoms of leukemia.

These things can be scientifically proven today. Such authorities as Karl Menninger and Paul Tournier have, in their writings, pointed out the connection between various cancer diseases and guilt. David knew it a long time ago by the Holy Spirit. Not all cancer is due to buried guilt, of course. But there was an obvious connection, according to David's own testimony, between his physical condition and his spiritual condition.

"My bones waxed old through my roaring all the day long," David admitted. The guilty person is often the noisy one in the crowd, the one who can't be quiet, the one who roars all the time, trying to cover up the noisomeness inside by noisiness outside.

"I loudmouthed it all day because I was so rotten inside, so guilty," David said.

"Day and night thy hand was heavy upon me: My moisture is turned into the drought of summer." David had such a high fever that his bones were drying up.

Body temperature is controlled by thermostats to stay around 98.6° Fahrenheit under normal conditions for most people. Sometimes, God lets the temperature go up higher to burn the bugs out of your system. But some germs refuse to be killed by a moderate fever. In pneumonia, your temperature might go up to 105° because those germs are hard to cook. At that point, you get out the aspirin and ice bags for your head because you don't want your brains to turn into mush.

Guilt and germs affect the body in much the same way.

Both of them can make us sick. That's why Jesus said, "Go and stop sinning, or a worse thing will happen to you." That's what He said to the man He healed at the pool called Bethesda (John 5:14). That's what He says to some of us, too.

About the time David couldn't stand his sickness any longer, God sent the prophet Nathan to confront him with his sin. Now Nathan knew all about David's sin, but he also knew that if he confronted David directly with the facts, he would hem and haw and make all the excuses he'd made all along. That wouldn't do any good.

So Nathan told David a story about the poor man who had had his one little lamb stolen from him by his rich and powerful neighbor, all because the neighbor didn't want to use one of his own animals for food for an unexpected guest. David heard the story and was roused to fury. The man would have to restore the lamb fourfold, he decreed, and he would have to die, because of his deed, and because he had no pity.

"You're the one," Nathan said. He gave the word of the Lord to David. David was convicted of his wickedness, and he confessed his sin to God.

"I acknowledged my sin unto thee," David says in the psalm. "My iniquity have I not hid. I said, I will confess my transgressions unto the Lord; and thou forgavest the iniquity of my sin."

As soon as David confessed his sin, God took away his buried guilt. With its corrosive action gone, David's bone marrow got nice and juicy again, able to produce all the red corpuscles he needed. David was healed.

Do you have any buried guilt in your life, iniquity you've

never acknowledged before God so He could get rid of it for you? Is there something you've never confessed to God, something for which you've never asked His forgiveness? You might get in worse shape than you are now if you don't get rid of it. Now is a better time than later.

Lord Jesus, thank You for opening my eyes to the iniquity in my life, the buried guilt I thought nobody could see. Thank You that my body has reflected it to get my attention to the ailment of my soul. Lord, thank You for fixing it so that I can't be deceived into thinking I'm nice when I'm not.

I confess all my sins to You right now. (NAME THE ONES HE BRINGS TO YOUR MIND.) Lord, apply Your cleansing blood to me. Bury my guilt and sin under that cleansing blood and make me whiter than snow in the blood of the perfect Lamb of heaven. Thank You, Jesus for paying the price for me on Calvary.

Let healing take place in my body now that I have confessed my iniquities to You. Let my body respond with health as my will becomes one with Your will. Make me whole now, in spirit, soul, and body, because I confess that I want Your will above my own. Forgive the iniquities of my sin just as You did those of David. In Jesus' name, let me be set free, let me be made whole. Amen.

"I could almost feel the power of Satan leering at me from the windows."

10

How to Be a Winner over Spooky Spirits and Dead Theology

And they overcame him by the blood of the Lamb, and by the word of their testimony. (Revelation 12:11)

One of the members of our prayer fellowship in Baltimore is a salesman who distributes thousands of tracts every week as he goes about his business. One day, the Lord led him to place a tract containing his own testimony on his boss's desk. The next morning, she sent for him.

"About that leaflet you put on my desk yesterday," she said. "I read it last night and was interested in your mention of something called the Holy Spirit. I know a lot about spirits, because I hold seances in my home every Tuesday night. But I don't know anything about this Holy Spirit. How could I find out something?"

"Well," Larry told her, "I could get someone to go over and speak to your group about the Holy Spirit. How would that be?"

"Fine," she agreed, and the date was set. Larry gave me the assignment.

I put on the full armor of God before I went to the woman's house. Unprotected, I'd have been a sitting duck. But I had every piece of equipment necessary for victorious spiritual warfare: the helmet of salvation, which is the blood of Jesus protecting my mind from spiritual invasion; the breastplate of righteousness, which is Jesus protecting my vital organs from the forces of darkness; the shield of faith warding off the fiery darts of the enemy that would otherwise cause my insides to deteriorate; and my feet shod with the preparation of the gospel (Ephesians 6:11-17). With all that, I could walk in and possess the land without any fear of harm to myself.

When I arrived at the house, I could almost feel the power of Satan leering at me from the windows. His presence was like a thick black blanket over the basement room to which I was ushered for the meeting. I was praising God constantly, praying in tongues internally, and I counted on that supernatural intercession going straight to heaven. Otherwise, I'd have been a goner.

At the beginning of the meeting, I was given an opportunity to witness for a few minutes to the twelve Jewish women sitting around in a circle. They were all locked up in the occult. I could tell that by looking at their eyes, by the gift of discerning of spirits. The devil leered hatefully at me from every person. He had recognized the arrival of a King's kid and knew he was headed for trouble.

At nine o'clock, the lady of the house said, "This is the time when we drop everything else and go into the silence to make contact with our friends." I knew the friends to which she referred were spooks, because I had been involved with such things once upon a time.

While the ladies went into their silence, I kept on praying in the Spirit.

After a prolonged period of rather unfruitful silence, our hostess spoke up.

"Something must have gone wrong tonight," she explained apologetically. "This has never happened before, but somehow, we've failed to make contact with the spirits. The other dimension can't come through for some reason."

•

Born losers keep their trade secrets, but they never know anything worth telling.
King's kid winners tell the good news all over town and get blessed.
•

If she had guessed that I was the reason, I might have been out on my ear. One King's kid in the enemy camp is a majority, and I had prayed Slue Foot right out of his own domain. Jesus, the Light of the world, had dispelled the darkness.

Following the silence during which they had waited in vain for something to happen, I was invited to continue with my testimony. Ordinarily, when I get to bragging on Jesus, I don't know when to stop, but the Lord stopped me this time after only a few minutes.

That's enough. This is the time. Ask her now.

I looked straight at the lady of the house and asked her the question the Lord had put in my mind:

"Did you ever wonder where that awful emptiness came from, that big vacuum inside you?"

The question had to come from the Holy Spirit. It certainly didn't originate in my think tank, because the lady didn't look empty at all. She was a successful business-woman, apparently happy—a widow worth millions. On the outside, she looked like she had everything to live for. On the inside, there was a God-shaped vacuum that kept her tormented and hungering for His reality.

"My awful emptiness? But how did you know? I tried to keep it concealed—" She dabbed at the corners of her eyes with a fancy lace-trimmed handkerchief that was plainly meant for decoration only. "It's driving me up the wall," she went on. "I've tried pills, I've tried alcohol, I've tried spiritualism—I've tried everything—"

I noticed that a couple of the other women were nodding their heads as if to say that that was their story, too.

"Would you like to have that emptiness filled? Would you like to have God's presence and peace in place of that awful vacuum?"

"Oh, yes!" she cried. "But is it possible for me? I'm an orthodox Jew. I was brought up in the Hebrew religion. This Jesus you talk about—I've been taught to blame Him for all my troubles, not to look to Him for answers."

"Lord," I prayed under my breath, "how can I handle this one?"

Before I could make a move, one of the other women spoke up.

"But didn't you hear what the man said, Esther? Jesus isn't a religion, so He can't conflict with your Hebrew training. He's a person, and this is a power hookup."

"Is it that simple?" Esther asked me, her voice full of hope.

"I guess so," came out of my mouth.

"Then that's what I want," Esther exclaimed. "I want the power hookup in place of this awful emptiness. What do I have to do to get it?"

> ## Our salt-of-the-earth testimony
> ## makes pagans thirsty for Jesus.

I was still thinking something complicated had to happen, that I would have to drag out John 3:16, Romans 10:9, and all the other standard steps to salvation. I figured no one could be saved without them.

But Jesus seemed to be saying, *Oh, no. I'm doing this one in a different way.*

I could see that He was, all right. The usual New Testament Scriptures would have turned the Jewish woman off. But testimony had turned her on. The Scripture Jesus put in my mind that day was not one for me to quote, just one for me to depend on. It went, "They overcame him—Satan himself—by the blood of the Lamb—the shed blood of Jesus that is ready to raise any corpse from the dead—and by the word of their testimony" (Revelation 12:11).

I could hardly speak. What Esther was asking could have been translated, "What must I do to be saved?" The Spirit of God had broken down sixty years of religious prejudice.

I moved a chair to the middle of the circle. Esther sat in it, I laid hands on her, and Jesus saved her and baptized her with the Holy Spirit—just like that. Her hands went up in the air, and she cried out, "Oh-h-h, Jesus! Thank You, Jesus! Praise You, Jesus!"

For somebody who had been taught to blame Jesus instead of to love and adore Him, it was quite an about-face. She turned to me and said, "I want to praise Jesus in Hebrew. Do you think that would be all right?"

"Jesus was a Jew," I said. "You can praise Him any way you want to, lady. He'll understand."

She began to praise somebody called Yeshua—that's Jesus in Hebrew—and then she shifted languages on me and praised Him in all sorts of tongues I could hardly keep track of. It was just like it must have been on the Day of Pentecost. No wonder the onlookers thought the disciples and their friends had had a little too much to drink. The wine of the Holy Spirit is pretty heady stuff.

For twenty minutes, Esther praised Jesus and thanked Him for saving her, for washing her in His own blood. The Holy Spirit, not flesh, had revealed these words and brought them through her, glorifying God in such a way that the other women could not fail to hear and be moved. After the Holy Spirit had scrubbed everybody's eyeballs for a considerable spell—and it's usually a sign that the Holy Spirit is busy when rivers of living water are overflowing like that—I asked a simple question:

"Who's next?"

Would you believe they all jumped up and stood in line for the prayer chair?

I asked Esther to lay hands on the first one and pray for her. It worked. Those two prayed for the third one. Those three prayed for the fourth one. Heaven was multiplied all over the place. All twelve former Jewish spiritists sat in the prayer chair and asked Jesus to come into their hearts and run their lives. Twelve out of twelve Jewish women gave their hearts to Jesus in less than two hours. Praise God.

I had done nothing to persuade them other than to give a briefer-than-usual word of testimony. I told it like it was with me. That's all. God did the rest, all by Himself.

Is there anything too hard for God to handle? He says there's not. If there is, I haven't encountered it yet.

Some of the women began to attend the local FGBMFI. I returned to the Tuesday night meeting at Esther's house a dozen times at her invitation—not to sit around and wait while they tried to conjure up spooks, but to conduct a New Testament Bible study so they could begin learning how to live like King's kids.

What have you been doing with the word of your testimony? Has it been mildewing in a desk drawer somewhere, or stuck behind your tonsils? Have you been too shy, too scared, too self-conscious, too full of pride to drag it out and let God use it to clobber the enemy and win somebody into His kingdom? Does the person who works beside you on the job know Jesus? Do you care enough to find out?

Yes, Lord Jesus. I know I've been guilty of concealing the powerful weapon You gave me. Forgive me for not using my testimony and everything else in my life to Your glory. Open the door for someone to hear, give me the boldness I need, and overcome the enemy in some lost soul's life this very day, using me.

Thank You, Lord, for Your powerful and enabling love. In Jesus' name. Amen.

11

How to Be a Winner over Bad Debts and Crooked Friends

Judge not, and ye shall not be judged: condemn not, and ye shall not be condemned: forgive, and ye shall be forgiven. (Luke 6:37)

How hard it is for those who have riches to enter the kingdom of God! (Luke 18:24 RSV)

About eighteen years ago, I loaned a considerable amount of money to a business partner. Let's call him Rodney. Over the years, Rodney prospered, because I turned my part of the business over to Jesus, and He really knows how to run things. In a short time, He had turned a struggling little company into three thriving corporations.

Over the years, every now and then Rodney made some kind of reference to the loan.

"Someday I'll get around to paying you," he assured me.

Well, I wasn't worried about the debt. I didn't need the money, so I didn't crowd him about it. Meanwhile, Rodney built himself a fine home, bought himself a yacht with his wife's name on it, and took vacations in the Bahamas—the whole prosperity syndrome.

A couple of years ago, we sold out our business and were both re-employed by the new owners. After I enjoyed four heart attacks in one month, it seemed prudent for me to get my earthly affairs in order so they wouldn't cause anybody undue concern if I suddenly took off on heavenly business. Accordingly, I got together with my attorney to do a little estate planning. Without it, I understood that the tax people would hog everything that otherwise might go into God's work on this planet. The government would use the money for everything *but* the spreading of the Gospel, and the church would use it to spread the good word about getting born again. The use the church would make of the funds I'd accumulated seemed the better bargain of the two.

While my attorney and I were working things out, I happened to remember the money Rodney owed me, a sum which ought to be included in the figuring.

Later, I called him, and told him that my attorney and I were working to get my affairs in order. "How about the money I loaned you eighteen years ago?" I asked. "Would it be convenient for you to pay it back now?"

Under the circumstances, I expected something like, "Sure. I'll have it to you in a few days." But that wasn't what I got. Instead, he seemed angry that I had asked him for the money. I could hardly believe it.

"You don't deserve it," he growled.

"Don't deserve it? Did I hear you correctly? You mean you

don't want to pay me?" It seemed a highly unbusinesslike
way to handle things.

He hung up without answering. That seemed even more
unbusinesslike. Inside, I started to seethe.

"That's my money," I fumed. "He borrowed it! What's he
mean by refusing to pay me?"

The longer I thought about it, the more miserable I got. I
didn't recognize that I was reacting to a pagan on his level
instead of kinging it up on the level where I was entitled to
live by virtue of my relationship to the Head of the universe.

A couple of days later, I was still partly under the
influence of my unrighteous indignation when I encountered
Rodney at the office.

"Have you made any arrangements about repaying that
loan?" I asked him.

He flew into a rage!

"You don't deserve that money!" he yelled. "I'm never
going to pay you! Go ahead and sue, but you'll never collect!"

●

*Born losers waste a lot of time trying to collect
their past-due accounts receivable—and go
broke with their goodwill all gone.*
**King's kid winners forgive their debtors and
prosper.**

●

He went into such a tizzy, I thought he would collapse on
the floor of the office. At that moment, the effect of my
martyr pills wore off, the hangover from my prolonged pity
party evaporated, and the Holy Spirit reminded me of something.

*Hill, you can be a loser or a winner in this situation. Take
your pick.*

He didn't need to say any more. I remembered what I had learned over and over again. If I insisted on being an owner, I'd lose. If I could relinquish ownership to God and just be a steward for Him, there was no way I could do anything but win. It was in the bag.

The Great Deception:
"You Can Make It without God."

"Praise the Lord!" I said, landing on the wavelength where I should have been roosting the whole time. "Rodney, I just realized that the money we're talking about is not my money. I want you to know that. It belongs to God, every cent of it. You'll have to account to Him for whatever you do about it. It's no longer my concern."

I turned to walk out, and all the seething and churning was suddenly gone from inside me. I was free from ownership once more, just like God meant for me to be all along. What happened about that loan was God's business and His alone. I wouldn't have to think about it any longer. As I continued to praise God for that, I felt ten tons of weight lift off my gizzard.

Rodney almost fainted. He looked white as leprosy. To be ready to fight and have your opponent pulled away from in front of you is an eerie feeling—like stepping down one more step in the dark when you've already reached the bottom of the stairs.

I said, "God bless you," and walked out. I was free. I could have cultivated an ulcer, gotten high blood pressure, arthritis, and all sorts of other undesirable adjuncts if I had insisted on remaining an owner in that situation. But when God, by His Holy Spirit, reminded me that to be a winner I had to be a steward instead of an owner, I was set free for my soul to return to prosperity so my body could remain in health, according to God's will for me as set forth in III John 2.

Possessiveness is a sure road to the kind of poverty that doesn't bring blessedness. Giving up ownership makes us richer all the time in all the things that matter. Willingness to be stewards puts us in a position of being ready for the next step in spiritual growth.

Today, I have no debtors. Nobody owes me anything. On paper, there are several people who are required to pay me varying amounts, but whether or not I get that money back is up to God, not me.

Does someone owe you something? Is it eating your heart out—giving you ulcers, ingrown toenails, upset stomach, dandruff, and heart palpitations? Would you like to turn it loose, be a steward instead of an owner and be set free? By the words of your mouth, it can be so this very day.

Lord Jesus, I confess to You this thing that has been eating at me, tormenting me, keeping me from partaking of the freedom You died to give me. (NAME THE SPECIFIC THING THAT'S BEEN BUGGING YOU.) Take it away. Make me a steward instead of an owner as I relinquish all my rights to You. And Jesus, please keep on working in me to make me like You are. In Jesus' name. Amen.

"Just then, an angel in a policeman's uniform drove up alongside us..."

12

How to Be a Winner over Traffic Jams and Time that Marches On

Have no anxiety about anything, but in everything by prayer and supplication with thanksgiving let your requests be made known to God. And the peace of God, which passes all understanding, will keep your hearts and your minds in Christ Jesus. (Philippians 4:6-7 RSV)

Whatsoever ye shall bind on earth shall be bound in heaven: and whatsoever ye shall loose on earth shall be loosed in heaven. (Matthew 18:18)

I started from my home about six o'clock one morning. My pastor, Peter Vroom, had picked me up to drive me to Washington National Airport where I was to catch a plane for faraway places. We were cruising along on the expressway about ten miles out of Washington when suddenly everything came to a screeching halt. Police cars, ambulances, and sirens all around us were a pretty good indication that there had been a highway accident up ahead.

Peter and I sat there interceding for the persons involved in the accident, and praising the Lord. We were already praised up and prayed up before we started on the trip, because King's kids can't afford to stop praising if they want heaven's best. We knew if we stopped praising for even a short time, we'd go under, because Satan would give us plenty of reasons not to start again once we'd stopped.

"Lord, this is Your trip," I reminded Him. "It's Your arrangement, for Your glory. It makes no difference to us whether I catch the plane or not. Whether I make the meeting or not is up to You.

"Frankly," I told the Lord, "I'd just as soon go back where I came from and crawl back in the sack. I wouldn't mind sleeping till noon. If You don't want to make this trip, it's all right with me."

That prayer did away with all my involvement in the struggle. Once I got rid of my selfish involvement, it was simply a matter of Matthew 18:18 going to work: "Whatsoever you loose on earth is loosed in heaven." I had loosed my concern and turned it over to Him. That meant that something wonderful was free to happen in the throne room.

It's as if God says, *Okay, little priests. Hang on as long as you can stand it. When it just about wipes you out, give up and I'll take over.*

After my pastor and I had loosed the traffic situation to Jesus, we sat there another twenty minutes. We were at a dead standstill physically, but getting closer and closer to heaven in the Spirit. Hallelujah!

We knew we still had to get through the whole downtown

area, past the Capitol, and down to the airport. Already there was no way I could catch that plane, and the clock kept on ticking the time away.

Thirty minutes were gone.

Thirty-five minutes were gone.

"Lord," I asked, my Bible in my hand, "do You happen to have any other special word for us today? If You do, please show it to us."

My Bible fell open to Psalm 107, and I began reading it aloud.

"O give thanks unto the Lord, for he is good: for his mercy endureth forever."

Wanting to be doers of the word and not just hearers only, we said, "Lord, we do thank You for all Your goodness to us—even for this traffic snarl, because we know that You can use it for good somehow. And we praise You that Your mercy never runs out, that it does endure forever."

"That's right," Peter added, "and I'm especially glad of that because we could use a little of that mercy right now."

My plane was to leave D.C. at 8:05, and it was after 7:00 already. The natural tendency was for the soul to panic, but God had us caught up in the Spirit, and the Spirit said, *Praise Jesus and keep on doing it.*

We kept praising Him, and I read the next verse.

"Let the redeemed of the Lord say so."

Peter looked at me, I looked at him, and we chorused, "Hallelujah, Lord! We're redeemed! Praise the Lord!"

The situation looked more hopeless than it had earlier, but we felt redeemed out of the hopelessness right in the midst of the locked-up traffic. I read on.

"Whom he hath redeemed from the hand of the enemy;

and gathered them out of the lands, from the east, and from the west, from the north, and from the south."

Sure enough, the cars had come from all directions, and they were bottled up at every intersection. Traffic was hopelessly snarled. Some drivers were driving their cars up on the grass in total desperation, frustration, and futility. As I looked around, I couldn't help but notice that the occupants of the cars around us looked pretty miserable. But I couldn't feel any misery in me.

"I wonder how many praising-the-Lord King's kids are in this mass of humanity here this morning," Peter said.

"Well, I know two," I told him. "But I don't see any others. They all look like disgruntled pagans. If they've noticed us, they probably think we're a couple of nuts."

"Screwed onto the right Bolt, though," Peter said, and I had to agree.

Reading further in the psalm, we were reminded of another time when King's kids were in trouble.

"They wandered in the wilderness in a solitary way; they found no city to dwell in."

Hey, that was us! We couldn't find the city either.

"Lord, that's right," we said. "We couldn't get into the city if we wanted to dwell there. We can't seem to pass through it to get on the other side, either."

Read on.

I did.

"Hungry and thirsty, their soul fainted in them."

More on-the-nose relevance to our situation! We were hungry and thirsty, all right. Neither of us had taken the time for breakfast, but our souls couldn't feel faint, because

88

we were praising. The sinking certainty that I had missed
my flight was overwhelmed by the fact that we were praising above the level of human reactions. We didn't have time
for a pity party.

**Nothing improves our
prayer life faster than big trouble.**

"Then they cried unto the Lord in their trouble," the
psalmist said. Well, trouble was where we were, and we
were crying to Him. God never promises to keep us out of
trouble, but He promises to deliver us out of it. You can't be
delivered out of something you're not in yet, so we were
exactly where God could bless us the most. We had trouble
to spare.

"Lord, this trouble must be a blessing, because You work
in everything for good. We don't see how You're going to
make all this turn out to Your glory, but we praise You
anyhow. This standstill must be exactly what we need."

Whatever else it might be good for, or not good for,
trouble will improve your prayer life. It invariably makes us
go caterwauling to the Lord. We might have forgotten all
about Him for a week, or for a month, but we get back on our
prayer bones in a hurry when trouble hits.

The next verse sounded exciting:

"And he led them forth by the right way that they might
go to a city of habitation."

"Hallelujah, Lord! Thank You that Your word is truth. It

looks like there's no way You can lead us forth by any way at all into the city of habitation where we need to go, but we praise You that You will do it because You said so."

That was exhilarating stuff. We turned our praises up a few decibels.

"Lord, we praise You for who You are, and for what You're going to do. Even if everything falls apart, we're going to keep on praising You."

•

Born losers gripe, grumble, nit-pick, and blame, and never get anything more for their efforts than secondhand leftovers from misery-land pity parties.
King's kid winners praise God in the midst of disaster and have heavenly feasting all the way.

•

Common sense wasn't along on our trip that day. Common sense would have said, "You blithering idiots. Can't you see what kind of a mess you're in? You might just as well have the satisfaction of grumbling, complaining, murmuring, griping, groaning, and blaming. All this praising and hallelujah business is ridiculous. You're just making fools of yourselves."

But we didn't want the second best benefits of common sense. We wanted the benefits of God's wisdom. So we persisted in depending on His word. Once again, I read on.

"Oh that men would praise the Lord for his goodness, and for his wonderful works to the children of men! For he satisfieth the longing soul and filleth the hungry soul with goodness."

We praised Him for his goodness and for His wonderful works toward us, works which we couldn't see yet, but works which we were counting on.

"Such as sit in darkness—" That was us. It was just barely getting daylight.

"And in the shadow of death—" That was us, too! The ambulances, sirens, and police cars proved it.

"Being bound in affliction and iron—" That was true, too. We were bound up in ten miles of Detroit iron.

My eye leaped to verse 13: "Then they cried unto the Lord in their trouble, and he saved them out of their distresses."

"Hallelujah, Lord! How are You going to save us out of our distresses?" I held the Bible up in the air so He could read His promise. "Lord, You wrote it. Thank You that You're delivering us now."

I closed the book and went to shouting. Peter was having a glory fit right along with me.

Just then an angel in a policeman's uniform drove up alongside us on the grass and began to funnel the traffic in our lane down a narrow little exit road off to the right.

"Lord," we said, "thank You that You've got us moving again, but we don't know where to go from here. We don't even know where we are."

We didn't have a road map, but He let us understand that we didn't need a road map when we had Jesus who is the way. That beats a road map any day.

Down the hill we spotted another man in uniform.

"How do we get to the airport?" we shouted at him.

"Second turn to the right!"

Seven minutes before take-off, I was on the plane. I can't tell you whether the Lord shortened the miles or lengthened the time, but I know He's able to do either one. My watch had said there was no way we could make it. But we did—with time to spare. And breakfast was served on the flight.

What do you have to do to reap the harvest of the benefits of God's promises? Plant praise. Cultivate praise. Watch it grow. Stay on the wavelength where God lives and moves and has His being. We are commanded to praise Him with every breath. He wants us to do that so He can bless us with every breath. Just as praise opened the avenue to the airport, praise opens the avenue for the blessings of God to flow in your life. That's King's kid living. Praise can turn born losers into born-again winners.

Have you been receiving the benefits of praise in your life, the blessings you enjoy when you turn all things over to Him and thank Him for everything? If you haven't, you can correct the situation by doing business with Jesus right now on His terms.

Lord, this sounds too way out for me, but I'm willing to be shown. I'm willing to learn. I'm willing to be trained to be a King's kid by Your Holy Spirit.

Thank You that You made us, that You know what makes us tick, that we couldn't have a more loving God than You are. Thank You, Jesus, for being You.

Lord, I'm so grateful that You chose me, You set me apart, You ordained and selected me before the foundation of the world. Thank You, Jesus, for every special arrangement You've ever made in my life. Thank You for every traffic jam You've broken up for me. Thank You for every time You've led me through unfamiliar streets and highways. Thank You that You're in the midst every time even two or three are gathered in Your name.

Thank You, Lord, that You can enable me, right now, to turn loose of everything I have bound on this earth, everything I have held onto in such a way that I prevented You from turning loose Your blessing for me.

Thank You, Lord, that You are always worthy of praise, no matter what the circumstances. Thank You that You are in charge of all the circumstances that You permit to come into my life.

Right now, Lord, I surrender and turn back to You everything I've been holding onto for myself. I thank You that, as a steward, I don't have to do anything but be found faithful, and that You can make me able to do that. Thank You, Jesus, that You have given us Your faith to live by. And thank You, especially, Lord, for making me want to praise You with every breath of my being. Amen.

13

How to Be a Winner
over a Bum Rap

Rejoice in the Lord alway: and again I say, Rejoice. (Philippians 4:4)

"The Spirit of the Lord God is upon me; because the Lord hath anointed me to preach good tidings unto the meek; he hath sent me to bind up the brokenhearted, to proclaim liberty to the captives, and the opening of the prison to them that are bound." (Isaiah 61:1)

In our town, a man found himself in court. The jury found him guilty, and the judge sentenced him to prison for twenty years. His wife came to our Bible study one night after he had been locked up.

"I have nowhere to turn," she said. "Our family is broken

up; our kids are ridiculed. Life is ruined for all of us."

She affirmed her faith in her husband's innocence, but the case had already been appealed to the highest court, and the judgment of the lower court had been upheld. There was no further legal recourse available.

"Do you suppose God could do anything to help us?" she pleaded.

"Well, there's one way to find out," we told her. "Let's ask Him."

She seemed agreeable to that. We prayed for her, she met Jesus, and He baptized her in His Holy Spirit. She was filled with such joy that she was praising God even though her husband was still locked up for half of forever with no hope of getting out.

"Now you're entitled to all the rights and privileges of King's kid living," we told her.

"What do I do to get them?" she asked.

"Just keep praising God," we said. "Praise Him because He says we are to praise Him. Praise Him for who He is. And while you're at it, you can praise Him for the mess you're in."

"Oh, I couldn't praise Him *for* the mess," she said. "I'd feel like a hypocrite."

"God isn't interested in how we feel about praising Him," we explained. "He just says we are to do it, no matter how we feel. He likes our praise so much that He comes to live in it when it's available to Him. When we don't praise Him, we create a housing shortage—a no-room-at-the-inn kind of situation—and make Him go back to that smelly stable—"

"Oh," she interrupted me, "I wouldn't want Him to have to do that—"

And so she began to say, "Lord, I praise You for the mess I'm in. Jesus, I thank You for it."

"That's a real good beginning," we encouraged her. "Try it some more."

She did, and when she really got in gear, thanking Jesus, the Spirit of praise began to take over in her. She sounded as if she meant every word she was saying.

> **Serenity is keeping your cool
> when caught in something you didn't do.**

Sometimes we have to begin by literally pushing the praises off the front of our teeth. If we keep it up by an act of will, pretty soon the praises are as deep as our palate, then as deep as our Adam's apple if we happen to have one. Eventually, the praise begins as far down as our navel, and finally as far down as the soles of our feet. That's when we start dancing in the Spirit, when our feet get into the act of praising God. And as everything that has breath in us begins to praise the Lord, our faith grows bigger and bigger. The woman with the imprisoned husband got into such a high gear of praise at our meeting that she began to believe God could do *anything!* Instead of wondering whether or not God could help her, she became bold enough to ask for something that was clearly impossible:

"Could we pray that God will get my husband out of prison in time for Thanksgiving?"

It was October already, and we knew there was nothing

we could do to get him out before doomsday twenty years hence. But she wanted him out in a month.

Could we pray that God would get him out in time to be home for Thanksgiving dinner with his family? Well, why not?

●

Born losers don't waste time on hopeless cases, and they lose the sure things.
King's kid winners tackle hopeless cases head-on and win them all.

●

"We have a big God," we agreed. "Let's pray a big prayer."

The woman sat rather hesitatingly in the prayer chair again. We laid hands on her rather hesitatingly, too, because that's a pretty big prayer for a guy who's been sent up for twenty years and all avenues of appeal have been exhausted. But we prayed it. And God heard it.

"Do you dare to keep on praising God without stopping?" we asked the woman.

"Is that scriptural?" she asked.

A quick look at I Thessalonians 5:16-17 persuaded her that it was scriptural, all right.

"But how can I pray without ceasing?" she said next. "I'll run out of words."

We laid hands on her again, and she got a new prayer language. She found herself suddenly equipped to pray in tongues without ceasing.

"Now can you rejoice evermore and in everything give thanks to God that your husband's in prison and there's no way humanly possible to get him out?"

She sounded determined, with a perfectly childlike attitude.

"Since God says it, I'll do it."

It may be tough to learn to be obedient, but it's highly beneficial when King's kids do it.

For two weeks, that woman praised God without stopping. At the end of those two weeks, the judge who had sentenced her husband to prison woke up in the middle of the night. He was nervous and couldn't sleep.

The judge was worrying about his decision in a court case. He got out of bed, put on his dressing gown and slippers, and went down into his study where he kept duplicate files of his recent cases. He pulled out the folder of the case that was troubling him, read through the record, and probably started talking to himself.

"I made a wrong decision in that one," he said. "I'll have to set it straight."

A few days later, the case was reopened at his request. Fred was set free from prison and exonerated of all charges. He wasn't home *for* Thanksgiving, he was home *before* Thanksgiving.

Have you ever thought of praising God for the hopeless situations in your own life or in the life of someone dear to you? Or have you been too busy with your pity parties to employ the most powerful tool God has given to His children? If you've settled for second best up to now, you can change over to God's best this very day as you open your mouth and begin to praise Him for things exactly as they are.

Oh, Lord Jesus, it is so good to praise Your name, to give

thanks to You. Forgive me that I so seldom use praise as a channel through which You can send me the blessings You died to give me.

Thank You, Lord Jesus, for Your forgiveness; thank You for the heavenly language You gave me when You baptized me in Your Holy Spirit. Thank You, too, for Your ability to plant in me the obedience to praise You with every breath of my being. Thank You, Jesus, for all You are to me. And now, Lord, I praise You for the very thing in my life that has been the greatest source of vexation and trouble to me. Lord, I do thank and praise You for (NAME THE THING FOR WHICH YOU HAVE NEVER BEFORE PRAISED HIM. THANK HIM FOR IT). Thank You for setting me free from all anxiety about this situation. Work in it to Your glory. In Jesus' name. Amen.

14

How to Be a Winner over Cirrhosis of the Liver and Little Faith

Confess your faults one to another, and pray one for another, that ye may be healed. (James 5:16)

And these signs shall follow them that believe; In my name . . . they shall lay hands on the sick, and they shall recover. (Mark 16:17-18).

Some years ago, eight of us non-practicing alcoholics were gathered together in one place, and one of us, whose name was Jim, said, "Now, tonight, we're going to have a healing service."

We were mostly too dumb to doubt, but we had a little bit of sense, and that's enough to delay the works of God sometimes.

"Is there anyone here who needs a healing?" Jim began.

Someone raised his hand and shouted, "I do!"

Jim sat him down in the hot seat, an ordinary chair moved into the center of the circle of chairs.

"Come on, guys," he said. "We're going to gather around our brother here and do just like it says in Mark 16. The four active ingredients for healing are a believer, a pair of hands, a sick person, and the name of Jesus. We're going to put the four ingredients together and see something wonderful happen. This guy is going to be healed."

At that early stage of my Christian life, I still had enough dependence on my Educated Idiot Box to make me dangerous, and I had also been exposed to dispensationalist theology, theology that dispensed with some of the most marvelous things of God and said they were not for today, that claimed that God's power petered out when Peter petered out. For those reasons, I couldn't go along with Jim without objecting a little.

"But Jim," I argued, "what about faith? Don't we have to have a lot of faith, too?" I knew God could heal today because He had healed my back at an Oral Roberts' tent meeting. But I was sure that Oral's faith had a lot to do with that, and I was equally certain that Oral's faith was a whole lot stronger than mine.

"Read it," Jim said, pointing to the Scripture for me. "Does it say anything about faith?"

I read it: "These signs shall follow them that believe. In my name . . . they shall lay hands on the sick and they shall recover."

"Does it say anything special about faith there?" he asked me again. "Does it say the believer has to be a spiritual giant for this thing to work?"

102

"Well, no," I had to admit. "But it does talk about faith in other parts of the Bible."

"Sure," he said, "it talks about fleas, flies, frogs, and the rest of the plagues of Egypt in other passages, too, but that's not what Jesus is talking about here, right? Here He tells us plain and simple that if a believer will lay hands on a sick person, the sick person will get well. Do you want to help or not?"

"But Lord," I was arguing inside myself, "what if I lay hands on him and we pray and he's not healed? What then?"

Are you afraid of ruining your reputation—or Mine? a Voice inside me seemed to ask. I was too chicken to answer. There was another way out.

I backed away a few steps and mumbled to Jim, "I'm sorry. I can't do it. I'm not worthy."

Theology teaches what man thinks God can't do.

But Jim didn't react as I thought he would. He laughed. "It's a good thing you know that," he said. "None of us are worthy. We're counting on Jesus' worthiness, not our own."

He had me look up another Scripture, this one near the end of the first chapter of I Corinthians. I saw there that Jesus Himself is my wisdom and righteousness and sanctification and redemption, and that if I was going to glory in anything, I would have to glory in the Lord. That kind of took the pressure off me and put it all on Jesus. Still, I was so reluctant that Jim had to take my wrists and move my hands onto the sick person.

Our patient was a big fellow with an advanced case of cirrhosis of the liver.

"Do you think God can heal cirrhosis?" the man in the chair asked when I had quit arguing.

"We don't know," Jim told him, "but now is as good a time as any to find out."

Even I could understand that if the cirrhosis went away then we could say that God is good at healing through ordinary believers. The man's cirrhosis was so advanced that it stuck out like a watermelon under his shirt, and he had his hands folded over the lump it made.

"You never heard of cirrhosis being healed, did you?" Satan whispered in my ear, reminding me that he was still around.

"Well, no, can't say that I have," I agreed with him. "But—"

"If I were you, I'd back away again. I wouldn't pray for a lost cause. Where did you get the nerve to pray?"

He almost had me backing down again, but suddenly I had the perfect answer for his question.

"I got my nerve out of the Book," I told him. "I can read. If it doesn't work, *you'll* have a testimony, but if it does, *I* will."

Jim knew the attack I was under, and he jumped in to settle it, once and for all.

"Slue Foot," he said, in a very commanding tone, "we're going to try this, and you'd better stand aside, ready to take off. Our God doesn't mention failure."

With that, we all laid hands on the man in the chair, and prayed simply, "Be healed in the name of Jesus Christ. Amen."

There was no hocus pocus, jumping, twitching, yelling, rolling, squealing, or hollering. There was no sign that anything had happened, either. But that wasn't our department. We had been obedient to do what the word of God said we were to do, and the results, if any, were up to Him.

•

Born losers say, "Seeing is believing," and never see much worth believing.
King's kid winners believe without seeing, just because God says so, and their eyes continually behold wondrous works.

•

Our patient looked down at his familiar bulge a few times during the course of the evening, but there was no change. He eventually went home, apparently in the same condition as when he came.

Well, none of us were surprised exactly. Just kind of disappointed.

The next night, he telephoned everybody, but I don't know why he bothered to use a phone. You could have heard him shouting halfway across Baltimore.

"It's gone! It's gone!" he yelled.

"What's gone?" We wondered if we were supposed to help him look for a missing object.

"My cirrhosis! It's disappeared!"

Wow! It had taken him fifty years of whiskey guzzling to grow that thing, and it had vanished in twenty-four hours. Glory!

"But why did it take a whole day to disappear?" a physician asked me when I told him about the miracle of healing.

105

"Why didn't God take the thing away immediately when you prayed?"

"King's kids are reporters, not explainers," I reminded him. "It's enough for us that God keeps His promises and gives healing to His children. Besides, when you consider that God takes nine months to make a little liver for a newborn baby, twenty-four hours is not bad at all for Him to make a healthy liver for a big man. And He had to take out all the old bad liver that was wrecked with cirrhosis, too."

How about you? Have you ever considered being obedient to lay hands on the sick that they might recover? You have nothing to lose but your pride. Amazing things continue to happen where King's kids take God at His word and do it.

Lord, You know I've never laid my hands on the sick and prayed that they might recover. I've never even thought of doing such a thing. I've never asked for prayer for myself, either.

Lord, I confess all this as sin in me, and ask You to make me obedient to Your word so that others might be blessed as You let Your power flow through my hands.

Thank You, Jesus, that You trust me with Your power. Please make me more available than I've ever been before to be a channel of Your blessing to Your people. In Jesus' name. Amen.

15

How to Be a Winner over Mortgage Foreclosures

Fear ye not, stand still, and see the salvation of the Lord, which he will shew to you today. . . . The Lord shall fight for you, and ye shall hold your peace. (Exodus 14:13-14)

And every one that hath forsaken houses, or brethren, or sisters, or fathers, or mother, or wife, or children, or lands, for my name's sake, shall receive an hundredfold, and shall inherit everlasting life. (Matthew 19:29)

In our church fellowship, there is a beautiful family—Don, his wife, and three daughters—who, from the time Don met Jesus, began to experience all kinds of problems.

It happens often. A man gets saved, prays, "Lord, use me," and right away all sorts of adverse things begin to come into his life.

107

Is this all accidental? Oh, no. God hears the prayer, "Lord, use me," and He sets about to make us useful. We're not usable at all until we have some experiences to share with others in terms of what God has done for us, how He has made His strength perfect in our weakness. When you experience God overcoming the impossible in your life, you have something worth sharing with a fellow sufferer. When he sees you've been through the fire yourself, he can't object that you don't understand. He knows you know how he feels. Paul says it in II Corinthians 1:3-4: "Blessed be God . . . who comforteth us in all our tribulation, that we may be able to comfort them which are in any trouble, by the comfort wherewith we ourselves are comforted of God."

The Living Bible paraphrase makes it plainer still: "What a wonderful God we have—he is the Father of our Lord Jesus Christ, the source of every mercy, and the one who so wonderfully comforts and strengthens us in our hardships and trials. And why does he do this? So that when others are troubled, needing our sympathy and encouragement, we can pass on to them this same help and comfort God has given us. You can be sure that the more we undergo sufferings for Christ, the more he will shower us with his comfort and encouragement" (II Corinthians 1:3-5 TLB).

Not long after Don was saved, he began to experience God's comfort in the midst of real tribulation. He had just signed a contract to buy a beautiful home out on the Severn River near Annapolis. He could well afford it, because he was a bright young man, highly trained, in perfect health, and he had an excellent job with all the best fringe benefits. His wife was employed, too, and they were enjoying abundant prosperity.

Then, the week after Don signed the papers and moved into the house, he lost his job. He was unemployed and overqualified. For three years, he looked everywhere for a job, and found none. Meanwhile, he fell further and further behind in making the payments on his home. Finally, the inevitable happened. The trustee of the second mortgage holder advertised the foreclosure sale in the Annapolis papers. It was to be held on the courthouse steps on January 13.

The humiliation of a public foreclosure was added to everything else. But Don and his family weren't humiliated. They had learned to praise God for everything.

> **Rest is release from ownership.**

When some of us prayed with Don as the date of the foreclosure sale grew closer and closer, a word of prophecy was spoken. The prophecy promised that in spite of the apparent awfulness of the situation, it would bring glory to God and victory to everyone involved.

I heard the prophecy and believed it, because it was plainly a word from God. But inwardly I wondered how He was going to pull this one out of the fire. Everything about the whole business looked downright grim. There was no way for victory to come unless God did a startlingly new thing.

If I had guessed how startling the events of the day were to be, I might have stayed at home where it was safe. As it was, half a dozen members of the prayer fellowship decided to be present on the courthouse steps on the day of the foreclosure to give comfort to Don and his family.

The day was the wildest of the winter. It snowed, hailed, sleeted, and rained. The wind howled and shrieked. Every kind of catastrophe the weather could throw at us, it did. We learned later that the storm was just a local one, and we had to believe it happened as a result of our praying up a storm.

Every real estate agent in his right mind—and all of them were, that day—stayed away from the foreclosure sale.

It couldn't have happened. This was choice waterfront property—sailboat dock with nine feet of water, separate boathouse with a drive-in underneath, huge apartment and fireplace above, 300 feet of deep waterfront, the grounds perfectly landscaped, everything in topnotch condition. It was exactly what real estate men would give their eyeteeth to handle, but not one of them braved the storms to come out.

The trustee was there, though, and he began the sale promptly at eleven o'clock in front of our bedraggled little gathering. The weather was so wild, we had to step inside the courthouse and hold the auction in the lobby. My pastor and several other kooks with me stood in the midst of certain defeat and praised God for the victory that none of us could see. We could see absolute wipeout instead.

There were no bidders except the second mortgage holder. He bid a measly $1000, and the auctioneer's voice rang out, "Going once, going twice—"

"Lord," I protested, "they can't do that. You can't let them walk off with that thing for practically nothing and hang a judgment on Don for the rest of his life—"

That's right, Hill, the Lord seemed to say. *Why do you*

110

think I brought you out on such a miserable day? Start bidding.

There wasn't time to argue. The trustee would have closed it in another split second.

"Five," I heard myself say.

"Lord, that's *thousands* they're talking about. I don't need this property—"

He agreed. *But I need it—for Don to live in—and I want you to bid for Me, Hill.*

After that, I had no choice but to relax and let Him bid through me.

•

Born losers own their own homes and struggle to make the payments.
King's kid winners let everything belong to God, and He supplies the greenery to make the payments.

•

When it was over, I turned to a lawyer friend of mine and asked him, "What did I do?"

"You just bought a $150,000 waterfront house for $100,000, that's what."

"I did?"

"Yeah, and you'd better hustle over to the bank and get your certified check—"

Two days earlier, I had received a five figure check as a down payment on business property I was selling. The morning of the foreclosure sale, I had planned to see my broker about investing the money, but God had sent me to the sale first—because He knew I'd need the ready cash to make a down payment on Don's home for him.

111

The trustee followed me in his car, and we closed the deal. I spent the rest of the day talking to bankers, lawyers, and real estate people about Jesus. I wouldn't have had that opportunity if I hadn't let Him get me in a financial predicament to start with.

Within less than a year, Don's wife received an inheritance that would have enabled him to pay me back for my investment and resume title to his property. What looked like catastrophe that fierce winter day had been filled with blessing because King's kids dared to trust the King.

Is there any area of your life where you've been holding on, holding on, holding on, refusing to let God take over and make you useful? Are you ready to relinquish it now, and begin to experience God's best for your life? It might be in the area of your job, your pocketbook, your children— Whatever it is, you can tell Him all about it and let Him make a fresh start for you.

Yes, Lord Jesus, I confess that I'm guilty of holding onto many things that I ought to turn over to You. (CONFESS THE SPECIFIC THINGS TO HIM.) And Lord, thank You for making me ready to do that right now. Please take my home, take my family, take my money, take anything and everything I have called my own—even my life, Lord—and use it however You choose, to the glory of Your wonderful name. In the name of Jesus I pray it. Amen.

16

How to Be a Winner over the High Cost of Flying and Hotel No-Vacancy Signs

Fear ye not, stand still, and see the salvation of the Lord, which he will shew to you today. (Exodus 14:13)

Several years ago, I was invited to participate in an International Christian Leadership Conference in West Germany. I prayed about it, and got a definite okay that I was to accept the invitation. The trip was by way of Paris and then on to Wiesbaden, Germany, where I planned to spend a week.

I made my reservation, got my passport in order, renewed my vaccination, and made plans to be away from my office for a couple of weeks. In the midst of the routine, I had a strange feeling about the whole thing, as if it wasn't going to be quite that simple. The circumstances seemed to warrant a fleece, so I could know for certain I was in God's will.

Some people say that fleeces are juvenile. Well, you'll have to call me and Gideon babies, then, because we use fleeces a lot.

"Lord," I prayed, "You know I want to be in the center of Your will in all this, so I'm asking You for a definite sign. If all arrangements continue smoothly, I'll take that as a sign the trip is Your will for me. But if anything happens to make the arrangements bog down in any kind of complication, I'll take it that I'm to cancel my plans."

Two weeks before we were to take off for Paris on Air France, I had a call from the Washington-based registrar of the trip.

"I have a change of flight plans for you," he began. "Instead of going by Air France direct to Paris, we have booked you to fly to Iceland, then to Luxembourg, and from there to—"

I had heard enough.

"Cancel me," I said. I explained to the registrar about my fleece, but he didn't exactly understand. He thought I was talking about some fur-lined overcoat or something.

"Are you crazy?" It wasn't a question the way he said it. It was more like a statement of fact. Well, that was his problem.

"It would seem that way to some folks," I replied. But if I hadn't honored the deal I had made before God, I could have been fogbound in Iceland forever. That happens.

Satan encouraged me to feel like a complete idiot. All the arrangements have been made to go and then Hill cancels out.

"Hill, you're a nut," he needled me. "You'll ruin your image if you don't go. You'll never get invited anywhere else, because they'll know you're undependable. Your reputation as a reasonably intelligent citizen will go slurping down the drain."

"Go away," I told him. "I'm going to play this one God's way and see what happens."

•

Born losers say, "God helps those who help themselves" (Hezekiah 13:13) and snatch defeat from certain victory without fail.
King's kid winners trust in the Lord with all their hearts and fervently pray, "God HELP those who help themselves."

•

Two hours later, my partner came in and told me that he had heard I had cancelled my trip. By a strange coincidence, he just happened to have a business appointment in England that he wasn't going to be able to make. All the arrangements had been made, and all expenses would be paid by the company.

"If you'd like to go in my place," he told me, "it'll take a week in London, two days in Stuttgart, and you'll be finished in plenty of time for your conference."

I'd get to make my trip—and it would be free. That sure beat staring at Icelandic icicles. I didn't try to stifle a "Praise the Lord" or two.

Before I left the states, the Lord dropped into my mind the name of an elderly Englishwoman my wife and I had met somewhere. I had no idea where she lived, but as I prayed, the name of another woman came into my mind, a Baltimore woman who might know the English lady's address. She did. With the address in hand, I made contact as soon as I arrived in England, and before the first week of my trip was over, the King had a new King's kid in the British Isles.

From there, I went to Stuttgart, took care of the company business, and headed by train for Wiesbaden. I had a phone number to call on my arrival, to find out where the ICL conference was being held and other necessary details. But somebody had goofed. The party who answered the phone had obviously never heard of me or the ICL.

I sat down in the railway station at Wiesbaden. I had no idea where to go, and no one to ask how to get there. All I had was Jesus.

Hallelujah! That would be enough. I got on the hotline to heaven, praying in tongues.

Consult a taxi driver. The Lord didn't say this to me in audible words, but by a strong impression that came into my mind.

"Lord, I didn't know that German taxi drivers spoke English."

You still don't. But go and find out.

I could afford to be obedient, so I walked out of the station to where the cabs were lined up waiting for fares.

"Do you speak English?" I asked the man in the first cab.

He just looked at me.

"Do you speak English?" I asked the man in the second cab.

He didn't even look at me, just kept staring straight ahead.

More cabs and more questions, and finally, one driver answered, "Yeah," in pure Brooklynese. I stated my problem.

"I've come over for a conference, but I don't know where

116

it's being held. Could you take me someplace where I could get a bed for the night? Then tomorrow I could find out what I need to know."

He shook his head.

"This is tourist season. There's an army post here. The UN is meeting just down the road at Bonn. There's not a hotel room anywhere, not even a stall in a barn. Everything's sold out."

"Everything?" It sounded unbelievable. "Are you sure?"

"You're the hundredth person I've turned down today." He sounded friendly, but convincing.

I had been continuing to pray in the Spirit while I was questioning him, and suddenly a word of knowledge fell directly from heaven. I was to ask the taxi man an outlandish question. His answer would be God's answer to me.

"If you were a stranger here," I said, "coming to this town to spend the night, and you could choose the best hotel, without having to worry about money, reservation, or any of that, which hotel would you choose?"

He mentioned one right away. I opened the door of the cab and started to climb in.

"If that hotel would suit you, it'll be perfect for me," I said. "Please take me to that one."

"But you don't have a reservation, do you?" He didn't start his motor, just turned to look at the crazy man in his back seat.

"No, I don't. Nothing about my circumstances has changed, but God has taken charge. Hallelujah! Let's go." I settled myself comfortably for the ride.

"But you'll be wasting your time," the cabbie insisted, making no move to take me anywhere.

Maybe he thought that somebody as crazy as I was couldn't afford the trip. I showed him some money—enough for my fare and then some. He shook his head, loaded my bags into the cab, and off we went. The back of his head looked as if he was thinking, "I have a real live nut this time." The real live nut was having a good time, however.

After a little, we pulled up in front of the most elaborate looking hotel I had ever seen. I got out of the cab.

"Would you take my bags into the lobby, please," I asked my driver. He was still shaking his head.

"Do you have a reservation?" he asked me again.

"No, I still don't have one, but this is where I'm going to stay." My answer triggered a repeat recital of his theology of impossibilities.

I listened politely, and when he came up for air, I asked him again to take my bags into the lobby. He was more than ready to have a sane customer for a change so he carried my luggage in, shoved my fare into his pocket, and took off. I wondered if he'd ever recover.

Meanwhile, I turned my attention to the lobby where two lines of people were clamoring for non-existent sleeping space. Was I supposed to join that elbowing, shoving, shouting rat race?

No. If you win a rat race, you are number one rat. King's kids can do better than that. I didn't join a line, I just kept standing there, praising the Lord with all that was within me. But the solution was nowhere in sight.

"Lord Jesus, I've gone as far as I can humanly go. This is it. What are You going to do?"

He showed me, right then. The elevator door opened directly in front of me, and out stepped Wallace Haines,

European secretary of ICL. I had met him in Washington a year or two before.

"What in the world are you doing here, Hal Hill?" he asked, pumping my arm.

Coincidence is when God works a
miracle and chooses to remain anonymous.

"It's kind of a long story," I managed to stammer out. "But the Lord led me here, and I'm hoping to find a bed for the night. Then tomorrow, I want to find out where the ICL conference is to be held."

"It's being held right here, believe it or not," Wallace boomed, pounding me on the back. "And you don't have to worry about getting signed up for a room. They're all filled up, I understand, but there's an extra bed in my room, and I'd be delighted for you to make use of it."

I didn't even have to bother to register.

"I'll be along in a minute," Wallace said, digging his room key out of his pocket and thrusting it in my hand. "I had just come down to get a paper from the newsstand."

All the way up in the elevator, I praised the Lord for His fantastic timing. It nearly blew my mind. And I should be used to His miracle-working ways by now.

There is nothing God can't do for King's kids who trust Him.

Are you ready to turn your unsolvable problems over to Him? Are you ready to praise Him right in the midst of the impossible circumstances in which you find yourself? To stop rushing madly about trying to do your own thing, trying to be number one rat in the rat race, and stand still so He can do His thing for you? If you are, praise the Lord and tell Him so.

Lord Jesus, forgive me that I've been so uptight, trying to run things my way when Your way is so much better. Make me slow down and look to You for all my needs. Make me to walk in Your Spirit that You might live Your victory in me.

Lord, let me glorify and praise You continually because You dwell in the praises of Your people, and I want You to dwell continually in me. I ask these blessings in Jesus' name. Amen.

17

How to be a Winner over a Shortage of Rental Cars

Be ye doers of the word, and not hearers only. (James 1:22)

Following the ICL conference in Wiesbaden, I prayed about whether or not I should rent a car to travel to Stuttgart, my flight departure point for returning to the United States. The Lord gave me a clear okay, so I telephoned the Hertz rental service. They spoke English. Understood it, too.

"I would like to have a car to drive to Stuttgart," I said.

"Fine," the voice came back. "When would you like to have it?"

"Tomorrow."

I could almost hear the Hertz representative shaking her head.

"Oh, but I'm so sorry. We're sold out for weeks ahead.

This is a tourist center, there is an army base, and the UN is meeting not far away. There's not a chance that we could give you a car any time this week."

Her story had a strangely familiar ring.

"Not a chance?"

"None. You would have to get on our waiting list at least two weeks ahead of time."

That sounded familiar, too.

"Are you sure about that?"

She was positive, so I thanked her very much and hung up the phone. Since there was no natural way I could get a car in time, I would have to depend on God's getting one for me in a supernatural way. He had managed to do the impossible so well in the hotel situation, I was looking forward to seeing how He would take care of this one.

The next morning, I packed my bags and went down to the rental office to get my car. No, I hadn't forgotten that the rental agent had told me there was no chance. God seems to work best in hopeless situations, and I like to have a ringside seat. He had told me that I was in His will to rent a car from Hertz for my trip. The rental agent could be mistaken, but God couldn't.

•

Born losers pay attention to what men say and drag through a limited life.
King's kid winners pay attention to what God says and enjoy the blessings of abundant life.

•

"May I help you?" the manager asked me when I had walked into his office.

"Yes, I'm here to pick up my car."

"Your name, please?"

I gave it to him, but added, "You won't find my name listed on your register of reservations, because I don't have a reservation with you." I wanted to tell him that I did have a reservation in heaven, but I thought that might confuse him.

"I'm sorry," he said again, and he looked really sorry, all right, "but it's quite impossible. There are no cars available just now. I'd be glad to put your name on our waiting list. Perhaps in a couple of weeks—"

"That's what the young lady told me on the telephone yesterday," I assured him. In the natural, he and I both had all the facts. But I wasn't depending on the natural. His theology about the impossibility of my getting a car that day only encouraged me.

| Jesus shows up best among shortages. |

My God is a God of the impossible, and He had given me a green light to drive a Hertz car to Stuttgart that very day, not two weeks later. All I had to do was to stand fast on His word, and the car would be forthcoming. But it was obvious the rental agent didn't have that information. I stood politely while he apologized some more. I was praising the Lord, of course, and I thought about how Moses had to lead the people to the very edge of the Red Sea before God made the dry path for them.

Suddenly the rental manager stopped talking. His eyes started growing wider and wider as if he couldn't believe what he was seeing right in the middle of the grassy green blotter on his desk. A set of car keys. He stuttered, stammered, and pushed his teeth back in. Then he reached out and picked the keys up.

"I forgot all about this cancellation that came in just a few minutes ago. My secretary hasn't had time to reassign it. Would an Opel be all right?"

"If it has four wheels and an engine, it'll be perfect."

I signed my name, he handed me the keys to the nonexistent car, I loaded my bags into it, and took off down the road. For all I know, the rental agent might be standing there still, trying to figure it all out. But I praised the Lord all the way to Stuttgart.

God had told me to rent a car. I didn't have to argue. I didn't have to take the manager's word for it when he said there was no car. I just had to stand and wait. All along, God had known something neither of us knew in the natural, and because I acted on His word instead of on the circumstances, He provided just what I needed.

Have you ever tried that? Have you been a winner because you looked at God and His promises instead of at the circumstances? Or have the circumstances claimed your attention, buffaloed you, and cheated you out of God's best for your life? You can turn around and claim your rightful inheritance any time you make the decision to do it.

Lord Jesus, I confess that I've relied on circumstances many times instead of acting on Your word. I'm sorry I've been so gullible about what men have to say and so unbelieving of what You have said. Lord, whenever there's a discrepancy between circumstances and Your Word, let me choose to believe You. Give me the faith to hold onto Your truth no matter what, and to act on what You tell me. Enable me to be a doer and not a hearer only.

Thank You that Your word is always true, though every man be a liar. Thank You that Your power *works* when we step forth and act on Your word. In Jesus' name. Amen.

Feelings are totally unreliable—they change with the weather.

18

How to Be a Winner
over Missing Your Turn

In all thy ways acknowledge him, and he shall direct thy paths.
(Proverbs 3:6)

How can we know the way? Jesus saith unto him, I am the way.
(John 14:5-6)

Before I set out to drive from Wiesbaden to Stuttgart in
the car that God had provided for me, I inquired as to the
location of the autobahn, the special superhighway on which
I would be traveling.

"Straight down the road," my informant told me. "Look
for a big wedgewood blue target on a pole. You can't miss it."

I thanked him and went forth confidently. I had temporarily forgotten what I've learned time after time. When anybody tells me that I can't miss something, I'm almost

guaranteed to prove them wrong. It happened again that day.

I drove further and further away from the city, down cobblestone roads that got narrower and narrower. This couldn't be the way to the autobahn! Suspecting that I had missed the sign, I pulled into a gas station yard to turn around. Parked at the station pump was a Chevy with a South Carolina license.

"Thank You, Lord. You must have an assignment for me here that I didn't know about. I praise You, Jesus, for letting me take the wrong road for the autobahn but the right road for You."

●

Born losers follow the road map for miles after endless dull miles in the wrong direction.
King's kid winners let the Lord guide them from one high adventure to another without a road map to spoil the fun.

●

I got out of my car and walked over to the Chevy to see what the Lord was up to this time.

Before long, I had learned that the man behind the wheel of the Chevy was a Southern Baptist missionary who was just starting a new mission church in Wiesbaden. He was so hungry for any kind of American Christian fellowship that for half an hour or so he let me tell him about the power hookup I enjoyed with the Head Man in the universe. It was the least he could do since I had traveled so far out of my way just to meet him. And the least I could do was to explain how the Baptism in the Holy Spirit *is* for today in spite of what he'd been told. By the time we parted, he *knew* there is something more beyond mere salvation.

"How do I get to the autobahn from here?" I asked him when we had come back down to earth, almost.

"Turn around and go straight back down this road," he said. "You can't—"

"Please don't tell me I can't miss it," I interrupted. "I already have."

"I think I know why, too," he grinned. "But this time, you'll see the big blue target, I'm sure."

He was right. God had just let me be blinded to it the first time because He had other plans for me at the service station.

After my divinely scheduled encounter with the South Carolinian who needed to know more about Jesus' provisions for King's kid living, I was soon on my way down the autobahn rejoicing at all the special arrangements God makes for His children to be blessed.

When it began to get cold and dark outside, and my gas tank was getting low, I looked at the map and realized that some further special arrangements were in order if one King's kid was to reach his destination. The map showed three exits from the autobahn into Stuttgart.

"Lord, which exit is the right one for me? If I take the wrong one, I could wind up in the Bavarian Alps or in East Germany. I'm not equipped for either one of them. You'll just have to show me which exit is the right one."

There were two out of three chances that I'd go wrong. My prayer life improved immediately.

"Lord," I petitioned Him again, "I know enough not to go

by my feelings, because that's not how You ordinarily navigate me, but in this case, I don't know how else You can guide me. Would it be okay for me to ask You to make the right exit 'feel' like the right one for me?"

He didn't say no.

> Feelings are totally unreliable—
> they change with the weather
> and what you ate for lunch.

I barrelled down the highway, past the first exit. It didn't feel right. As I approached the second one, I reminded Him, "Please let me feel it strong and clear if this is the one." There was no special leading as the distance narrowed down, so I kept my foot on the accelerator and kept going. The third exit loomed, and right beside it a huge Esso sign, red, white, and blue.

"Now I'll get oriented," I told myself. Then I remembered that attendants at Esso stations in Germany speak German instead of red, white, and blue English. I didn't know a single word of German. This was inconvenient, since the roads branched in six different directions from that exit.

"Lord, You see how helpless I am. Please give me one word of German. Just one." I thought I probably had faith to receive that much.

When I had finished my prayer, the Lord flashed a big sign with gold letters in front of my eyes. I saw the letters B-A-H-N-H-O-F, but I didn't know if they spelled a word, or if they did, what the word meant. I confessed my bewilderment to the Lord.

"Lord, thank You for those letters, but they won't do me a lot of good unless I know what they spell. What are You trying to tell me? Could You clarify it just a little bit?"

The sign expanded into a clear picture of the railroad station directly across from my hotel in Stuttgart. *Bahnhof* must mean *train station!* That was all I needed to know. The perfect word.

When the gas station attendant approached my car, I indicated by signs that I wanted him to fill the tank. Then I asked him, Indian style, "How Bahnhof?" thinking he'd understand that abbreviated form better than a more complicated, "How do I get to the Bahnhof?"

He said a bunch of things I couldn't understand, but he pointed down one of the six roads, and I headed that way. Just a few hundred yards down the road, I came upon a man walking along, carrying the biggest suitcase I had ever seen. The Lord told me to pick him up, so I did, figuring he would be able to speak English or German fluently. Well, he didn't speak either one, but the Lord had His reasons. He did seem to know the one German word I knew, because when I said, "Bahnhof?" he nodded his head vigorously and lit up like a Christmas tree. I gathered that he wanted to go to the Bahnhof. Since my hotel was directly across the street, we were perfect traveling companions for each other, language barrier notwithstanding.

I indicated to my passenger that he was to roll down the window on his side of the car and call out, "How Bahnhof?" to likely looking pedestrians along our route. From then on, we went straight or turned, according to their pointings, and eventually pulled up in front of my hotel and the railroad station.

When he got out of the car, my passenger took his wallet

out of his pocket and opened it, gesturing to ask me how much he owed me for the ride. I just shook my head and praised Jesus for the fellow who didn't seem to realize he had done me a big favor by riding along.

Later, when I was recounting my German adventures to an American who could speak German, I learned that my Indian "How" had been part of the miracle. In German, the word "Haupt," meaning "main," is pronounced something like our word "how." When we said "How Bahnhof?" we were asking directions to the main train station in Stuttgart—and there were five other ones. Without our Indian talk, we could have wound up at any of five different *wrong* train stations, instead of the right one across from my hotel. Glory to God? And how!

Believe it or not, I have never deliberately, knowingly prayed that God would get me in trouble. But He seems to do that anyway, sometimes, without my asking. As long as I am prayed up and in a high gear of praise, everything turns out better than if I hadn't gotten into trouble to start with. God's simple directions to praise Him continually, no matter what, are what makes the difference between panic and victory.

Have you been a winner when trouble strikes, when plans aren't laid out nice and clear? Or have you reached for the panic button? Have you been able to get through impossible situations, trusting God to guide you, praising Him in the midst of uncertainty or confusion? Or have you given way to confusion yourself? Jesus died that you might have total victory in every area of your life. Have you been settling for less?

Are you willing for Him to take you out of your way so He

can do something through you for another one of His children? If you are willing, you can get an assignment by putting your name in the pot. But don't do that unless you mean it.

All you have to do to turn from failure to success while you wait is to get tuned to God's wavelength, to get on and stay on His channel of praise.

Lord Jesus, forgive me that I have always thought I had to plan every step of the way for myself. Forgive me that I've always had everything so carefully laid out for myself that there was no room for You to guide me. Lord, I confess all this as sin. Do change me. Make me depend on You instead of on me. Help me to know that You're the author of all blessings in my life, and help me surrender more and more of it to You. Handle everything in my life exactly as suits You from now on. Show me the road You want me to take for Your glory. Thank You, Lord, that You can make a winner out of me, in spite of my do-it-myself nature. And thank You, Jesus, that You have made me willing to go out of my way to let You do something through me for one of Your needy children. Use me, Lord. Use even me. Amen.

"Up that path came a barefooted country boy with ragged britches and an old straw hat..."

19

How to Be a Winner
over Anxiety

Follow me, and I will make you fishers of men. (Matthew 4:19)

Once upon a time, I was with Tommy Tyson when he was preaching a revival in a Methodist church in Grand Rapids, Michigan. As the week drew to a close, Wayne McLean joined us. On Saturday, Tommy made an announcement.

"There àre three of us," he said, "and we have three speaking invitations for Sunday morning. I'll take one church here in Grand Rapids, Wayne is taking another one, and Brother Hal, that leaves a pulpit in Plainwell for you."

Well, pulpit sharing was something I hadn't gotten into a whole lot at that stage, and it was kind of scary to me. The prospect of what I supposed would be a small country church instead of a big city cathedral calmed my nerves a little bit, however, and I figured that maybe the Lord and I could handle the assignment.

When I arrived in Plainwell, my butterflies started galloping again, because I learned that there was no little country church on the menu. I was to speak in the big downtown Methodist establishment. As I peeped into the auditorium, it seemed to me that it would probably hold at least seventy-five thousand people. It was a wonder that I didn't faint dead away before the choir finished singing the doxology. I certainly felt almost like doing just that. But along with the apprehension, there was a sense of anticipation in me, too, precisely *because* I was so ill-prepared as the world sees it.

When I'd climbed into bed the night before, I'd prayed, "Lord, I don't have a thing to offer as a pulpit occupier, because I'm not a preacher. If I were, I still wouldn't know what to say to a Sunday morning congregation. You'd better cancel me out, Lord. I don't think we ought to go through with this thing. I might let You down. You really ought to find somebody else. Please?"

As far as I could tell, He didn't answer yes or no, and eventually I went to sleep. Then I must have wakened, because I had a clear vision from the Lord that night. It was far too vivid to be a dream. It went like this:

I was standing as an observer at the site of a big fishpond. Fishermen were whipping up foam on all sides of the pond with all kinds of fancy fishing gear. Their waders and accompanying outfits to match had to be from Abercrombie and Fitch. With all that high-class equipment, they were fishing for all they were worth, but they were catching nothing, not even old shoes or inner tubes. They were having the dullest time imaginable. As they worked harder and harder, they reeled in more and more of nothing. Their creels were full of empty space.

Suddenly the scene changed.

All the fishless fishermen turned their eyes down a path leading into the woods. Up that path came a barefooted country boy with ragged britches and an old straw hat. Over one sun-freckled shoulder, he had slung a branch off a tree for a fishing pole. It had a piece of knotty grocery store string tied to it for a line, with a bent safety pin hook on the end of it. In the other hand he swung a battered galvanized bucket.

As the boy approached the pond, he was whistling a lively tune that sounded like an invitation to a heavenly fish fry. All the fancy fishermen stood watching him with looks of utter disgust on their faces that said, "What's this clown think he's going to accomplish? Nothing's biting today—can't he see that?"

But the boy paid no attention to the impossibilities that were so obvious to them. Still whistling in perfect confidence, he reached into the bucket he had set down on the bank. Just as you might have expected, he drew out a piece of bait and squirmed it onto the bent pin hook.

There wasn't anything at all unusual about his actions. Barefoot Huck Finns of every age have gone through the same motions billions of times. But the bait was unusual, like none I'd ever seen before.

The bait was a piece of glory. Now don't ask me what a piece of glory is, and don't ask me to describe it. The important thing for a fisherman who wants to take home a catch is not what the bait is, but what it does. This bait did the trick.

When the boy cast his glory bait out into the water, the glory lit up every inch of the pond with a silvery glow that looked alive! After he had tossed in his bait, the boy just stood and waited, still whistling. The disgusted onlookers stood and waited with their mouths hanging open, expecting nothing to happen. I stood and waited, too. But none of us waited long.

Suddenly, out of the shadows of that fishpond came a huge lunker—must have been a four or five pound largemouth bass—headed slowly but surely straight for the bait. The prize catch sniffed at the glory, opened his wide mouth wider still, and closed down over it. The boy eased the fish to the bank without any struggle, and put the perfect fish into his bucket. Then he threw his glory bait back into the pond. This time, I saw shadows in the water coming from all directions.

The onlookers' eyes got bigger and bigger, and their disgusted looks were transformed into expressions of awe and wonder.

As I watched, the Word of the Lord came to me and said, *It is not the fisherman. It is not the equipment. And it is not the willpower or the determination. It is My Word, and My Word alone, that does the job. If I be lifted up, I will draw all men unto Myself.*

•

Born losers spend years and fortunes getting themselves "qualified"—to do nothing.
King's kid winners recognize their only qualification is knowing Jesus, and that qualifies them for whatever opportunities He sends their way.

•

The ordinary bucket was soon full of extraordinary silver fish, and the boy picked it up and went whistling back where he came from. The fancy Dapper-Dan do-it-myself fishermen stood like statues, transfixed by what they had seen. I wouldn't be surprised to learn that they are standing there still.

The vision never closed for me, exactly. I can see it vividly today. It keeps on reminding me, *It's not you, Hill. You don't have to be anything. You don't have to amount to anything. You don't have to do anything. My Word does the whole thing. Just toss out My Word, like the boy tossed the glory bait into the water, and I'll do the rest. Just as inevitably as the fish were drawn to that glory bait, I'll draw all men unto Me.*

All that was fresh in my mind the next morning as I stood in that high pulpit of the big Methodist church. Standing before the people, I could see the Word of God coming down from heaven on a track off to my right. The track brought the Word directly into my head from the Lord, and out my mouth, as directed by the Lord. He was in charge of every word of it, plus the delivery, the punctuation, and the pauses.

**God ministers His Word, by His Spirit,
through His disciples,
for His glory and our blessing.**

While I was pouring out what He was pouring in, I saw in the Spirit a huge block of marble on the pulpit right in front of me. It must have been two or three feet square, a cubic hunk of pure white. As soon as I had spotted it, the Spirit seemed to say, *Hill, push that marble off the pulpit. I will make it land on someone in the congregation.*

If I hadn't been so busy pretending to preach, I might have thought of several good arguments against that course of action.

But I was too busy letting the Word flow through me to do anything other than follow His instructions in simple obedience. I got my shoulder under that marble block—the congregation must have thought I was having muscle spasms—shoved with all my might, and the block fell with a huge crash somewhere down below, in the midst of the assembly.

Apparently I was the only one who heard it land, because no one else moved a muscle. All this was going on in the Spirit while I was delivering the Word as it was delivered to me. When my allotted speaking time was up, I sat down. "What hath God wrought?" I wondered.

After the service, I found out. A white-haired woman came to me said, "I have been in the Methodist church from infancy until my present age of eighty, and this is the first time I have ever heard that I could know God personally. And now I know I can, because I do. I met Jesus this morning, in person."

We had a glory fit right there in the midst of churchianity.

Praise God that it's not by might, it's not by power, but by His Spirit, saith the Lord. It's not the fisherman, it's not the equipment, it's the Word of God that gets the job done. His Word is the glory bait that makes us fishers of men—with a catch to show for our labors.

Are you ready to trust Him that He can send the Word forth through you and accomplish something wonderful for one of His children who needs to know Him personally? All you have to do is say so.

Lord, I *am* ready to trust You that You can send Your Word forth through me and accomplish Your purpose with it. I thank You for bringing me to this point in my life today. Show me the one who is ready to receive You, Jesus, and open my mouth and speak through it for Your glory. In Jesus' name. Amen.

20

How to Be a Winner over Ungodly Spirits

And these signs shall follow them that believe; In my name they shall cast out devils. . . . (Mark 16:17)

I was at a CFO camp in Hastings, Nebraska, one summer. The song leader was a big boy, football-player build, who had been saved and filled with the Holy Spirit the preceding year. He had been so full of joy that when his friends saw him the summer I was at camp, they hardly recognized him.

I myself had never seen anyone more depressed and discouraged. His complexion was sallow, there was no joy in him, no inner light, no peace. Everything that had made him glow with life was completely gone.

Some of us on the staff began to pray, "Lord, what is it? Minister to this boy the abundant life You died to give him. Show us what we can do to help."

The next day, several of the boy's friends brought him to our CFO Council Ring for counseling.

"I don't understand what's wrong with me," he muttered, looking down at his shoes. "I've lost all my enthusiasm. I feel incapable of doing anything for myself or anybody else. I feel like I can't go back to college this fall. I can't study, I can't do anything."

At that point, he lost control of himself and began sobbing, "I can't —I can't—I can't—" over and over again. His big hulk heaved with the agony of helpless defeat.

Finally he looked up at the other two staff members—Jim Christian and Willie Murphy—and at me.

"Help me," he cried out. It was a desperate cry.

"There's no way in the world that we can help you," I told him, "but we know Someone who can."

A brief flash of hope crossed his face. He knew I was talking about Jesus, the only One who can really help us with anything.

I had been praying in tongues as the boy was pouring out his problems, and as I prayed, I had seen a demon of despair in him. That demon was responsible for the boy's desperation. The demon would have to go.

"Would you like for all of us to pray for you?" I asked him.

The boy had nothing to lose—except the demon he needed to be rid of—and so he walked over to the prayer chair and sat down.

The three of us laid hands on him and began to pray. When we did, the demon went wild. In spite of all we could do, the boy—all three hundred pounds of him—was thrown to the floor, where he hissed, squirmed, and writhed like a snake. In the midst of all that, the demon began to shriek. All in all, it was one of the wildest scenes I'd ever gotten into.

Jesus has given Christians authority over the powers of darkness, and so we began to speak it out: "Satan, in Jesus' name, come out of him."

"I won't! I won't!" the demon screamed through the boy in a defiant voice utterly unlike the boy's own. "You can't make me go. The boy invited me in. This is my home. This is where I'm going to stay."

We didn't have to argue with him. We just told him the facts.

●

Born losers run from the devil, trip, and get caught.
King's kid winners use Jesus' power to make the devil run from them and do his own tripping.

●

"Satan, you're a conquered foe. Jesus has already conquered you, so you don't have any choice in the matter. You have to go. In Jesus' name, we command it."

We bound the demon in the name of Jesus and ordered him back to the pit where he came from. Suddenly, the boy's body relaxed. He was not contorted and writhing any longer, and we knew the demon was gone. Jim, Willie, and I stood up—we had been down on the floor with the boy—and gave him a hand. He sat back in the chair again, apparently free from despair but exhausted from the struggle. Sweat was pouring off him. As we continued to pray in the Spirit, the Lord gave us a clear warning:

Check further. There's another one, another foreign spirit inside this boy.

"Reveal yourself, demon. What is your name?" The demon knew we had spotted him. Trying to hide from us would be a waste of time.

"Lysergic acid diethylamide," he answered. In the Spirit, I could see the word spelled out, and knew it to be the spirit of LSD. The spirit was white as snow, just like the spirit of leprosy in the Bible. I saw that the LSD drug of leprosy of the soul had two big white hooks jabbed right into the soul of that boy.

We learned later that he had taken an LSD trip after he was saved. He had had a bad trip, and afterward had been plagued with an unending series of random returns or flashbacks, all terrifying. He never knew when to expect one. Slue Foot had sent them at varying intervals to keep the boy in constant fear and suspense. I knew that God had revealed that demon to us for one purpose. He meant for us to deal with it and set the boy free.

"Spirit of LSD, we bind you in the name of Jesus Christ. Come out of him."

> Jesus will change you
> from an ungodly mess
> into a Godly message.

That was all there was to it. We heard a popping noise, like a cork coming out of a jug, and the boy's face began to shine with the glory of the Lord. Jesus had delivered him of two demons, cleaned him out, and refilled him with joy.

Drugs are likely to be inhabited by demons, and when you

take a drug, you might be swallowing a demon spirit which will make you so miserable, you'll wish you'd taken a deadly poison instead. But King's kids are equipped with the tools to get people delivered from demons. Jesus expects us to use them to set His people free.

The gift of discernment of spirits is one by which we can see exactly what it is that is keeping a fellow Christian from being a winner. The Lord can reveal these things to us as clear as photographs.

You don't get readouts like that? I didn't either, back in the days when I wasn't letting Jesus have first place in my life. I didn't have this supernatural help in ministering His life to His children until I had learned to put away all second best in my own life. That meant that all unforgiveness, impatience, unteachableness, and unbelief had to go. The television set had to go, the bridge clubs, the chess clubs. Even good things had to move over to make room for the best, because the effect of the "good things" was to fog the signals from heaven.

Secular TV is the worst offender, because people have a tendency to think "It's not *all* bad," and they unwittingly expose themselves to garbage-can scum along with the "goodies" of moon shots and Sunday morning sermons. If you're a TV addict, you might like to read your version of the twenty-third psalm to see why God isn't making more use of you in ministry:

The TV Addict's Twenty-Third Psalm

The "Tube" is my shepherd; I shall not want for filth. It maketh me to stare stupidly at its putrid perversion; it leadeth me into the polluted waters of degradation. It poisoneth my soul. It leadeth me in paths of violence for Satan's sake. Yea, as I walk through its portrayal of sin and death, I shall fear every evil, for its loathsome lewd eyeball discomfits me. It prepareth a table of corruption before me in the presence of my lost friends. It anointeth my head with raw sewage; my stomach turneth over. I devour more pills. Surely torment and fear shall haunt me all the days of my life, and I shall dwell in the pits of despair forever.

Another thing to remember in casting out demons: They are not deaf. In the beginning of my life as a King's kid, I'd carry on in a loud voice, whistle, holler, curse Satan, and stomp his tail when I wanted to get rid of him. I'd seen some folks do these things, and I thought I had to scare Satan to death with a loud racket in order to get him to pay any attention to my commands. But I learned that was a childish way.

Satan doesn't depart because we shout at him. He departs because Jesus has conquered him and given us the authority to remind him of that fact. The noisy way was an amateurish way. "When I became a man, I put away childish things," Paul said. It is appropriate for us to do it, too.

In the Belvedere Baptist Church in Baltimore, we have a concrete masonry prayer room with no windows. The demons being cast out get noisy sometimes, and we don't want to scare the whole neighborhood. It's logical to expect some complaint from the boys in black when they're ordered off the premises where they've been so comfortably ensconced. The demons don't come out whistling Dixie, but they do come out. They have no choice when a King's kid uses the authority that Jesus has given him.

Are you ready to be used in the kind of ministry that sets people free from demonic oppression? If you want to minister in the Spirit, delivering God's best to His needy children, you have to lay down your life and be sold out to Jesus. Only in that way can you be His channel for maximum benefits to needy people.

Have you renounced all the roadblocks to God's power flowing through you—all the impatience, unbelief, unteachableness, and unforgiveness? Are you willing to renounce all the temptations of the occult—horoscopes, Ouija boards, seances, and predictions of false prophets? Are you willing to give up all preoccupation with second best—bridge clubs, chess clubs, sports events, six-packs, goofballs, and television—in order to be used in more powerful ways as a conveyer of God's blessings to His people? If you are ready, God is willing.

Lord, cleanse me of everything that is not part of Your highest will for my life. Lord, make me a proper vessel, fit for Your use.

Lord, here am I, send me. In Jesus' name. Amen.

"There's no such flight."

21

How to Be a Winner over the Frustration of Fouled-Up Flight Plans

Rest in the Lord, and wait patiently for him. . . . (Psalm 37:7)

I had been invited to talk to the congregation at a Christian conference. Accordingly, I called my travel agent, gave him the details of my itinerary, and a few days later, my airline ticket arrived in the mail. I recognized the envelope, so I didn't bother to open it, because I was trusting my heavenly Father for the proper reservations. I don't have to check up on Him.

That my reservation had been made for a flight that was nonexistent didn't disturb me, because I didn't know about it. If I had known, I might have worried, gotten concerned and called my travel agent. But I didn't know, and so I went along in blissful ignorance.

On the appointed day, I left Baltimore for Tampa by way

of Jacksonville. It was a short trip with practically no layover, I thought. When I got to Jacksonville, I went to the airline counter to reconfirm my ticket for Tampa. The attendant took my ticket from its envelope and frowned at it and at me.

"There's no such flight at 2:30 this afternoon," he said. "That flight was dropped weeks ago. We don't have a flight to your destination until six-thirty this evening."

My first reaction was impatience—and annoyance—at my travel agent.

"When I get back to Baltimore, I'll fix that so-and-so. I give that guy a lot of business, and he does this to me—" Oh, I really seethed inside. Who were they to interfere with my plans?

But before I could get up a full head of steam and give vent to my natural reaction, the Lord seemed to say to me, *Now wait a minute, Hill. Why have you stopped praising Me? What have you been preaching? Haven't I heard you talking about praising Me for everything?*

He had me there.

> Pagans have bad luck—
> King's kids enjoy adventures.

"All right, Lord, I acknowledge that You've probably got a purpose in allowing this to happen. The fact that I don't know what it is is beside the point. And even if I never know why You let it happen, I should be praising You anyway. I do praise You, Lord. I thank You for this delayed flight. I thank You for whatever You have in store for me at this airport. Thank You, Jesus."

It made me feel better already, getting off the griping frequency and tuning back into the praise frequency where God has His habitation. I let the man write me up a ticket for the six-thirty flight, and I called the conference leader and explained that I was on my way but that I'd be a little late. It didn't seem to matter all that much to him. They'd get along fine without me.

Next, I telephoned everybody in the area I could think of who might be able to come down and praise the Lord with me in the extra hours while I waited. But filling the hours that way must have been second best to what the Lord had in mind, because I didn't find any takers. It was the best thing I could think of, but my best is never better than heaven's second best. I decided I could afford to wait for Him to make the next move.

●

Born losers never just sit there, they do something. It invariably makes things worse.
King's kid winners rest in the Lord and wait patiently while He makes all things work together for good for them.

●

After tending to those details, I just sat down in the airport and praised the Lord and sloshed around in the Scripture for a while. Then I ambled into the coffee shop, and did a little exploring of other parts of the terminal building. The airport was a big, beautiful, new one, with a lot of things to see, so I wandered around ogling everything. My antennae were unfurled in case there were any signals I ought to pick up. I wanted to put my hands in the air and praise God, but there were a lot of folks in the airport who

153

might have misunderstood and called the men in white, so I kept my hands in my pockets. But deep down inside, I was praising God in my prayer bucket to stay on God's wavelength and receive His signals from heaven.

"Lord, I'm rejoicing evermore, praying without ceasing, and praising Your Holy name," I told Him. "That makes me Your will in action. What do You want me to do?"

While I was talking to God, Satan kept trying to get a word in.

"Hill, you're wasting your time. You should be at your destination already. Don't you need to chew your fingernails or worry a little bit? How about one for the road? Maybe you could crank up a pity party—"

"Go away, Slue Foot. You can't discourage a King's kid when he's praising God."

Continuing my strolling through the terminal building, I noticed a sign that said "Chapel."

I'd never seen a chapel in an airport before, so I headed in the direction of the arrow. It wasn't far to the chapel, and soon I was there. I walked into the little sanctuary and sat down to read some Scripture and to praise God out loud. Since I was the only one in the place, I even felt free to let my arms get vertical overhead.

After I had enjoyed the presence of the Lord thusly for a few minutes, the door opened and someone looked in. "Come on in," I called out, thinking I might have some fellowship while I waited. A man and a woman came in, and I asked them, "Are you folks religious?" (Religion has to do with what God can no longer do. Religious theology explains in detail why He can no longer do certain things. A Christian, on the other hand, is someone who knows Jesus personally and can't help but brag on Him.)

"No," the woman said, "we're Christians."

Right away, things were looking up.

After I understood that this couple was more than ordinary church folks, I said, "Well, I'm a Christian, too. I know Jesus as my Savior, Healer, and my Baptizer."

"Hallelujah!" the man said. "That makes three of us."

Now we were in business. King's kids had met with King's kids in the chapel. I knew it was a divine appointment, arranged in heaven, because I had God's promise in II Corinthians 5:18 that all things are of God.

Well, when my heavenly Father says I'm not in a particular place at a particular time by accident, but that my being there is of Him, I'm interested in finding out what He's up to. As I talked with the couple, I began to get an inkling.

The young woman, whose name was Betty, said, "My sister's flying in from Atlanta this afternoon. She's going into the hospital for surgery. The doctors don't know whether she has a malignancy or not, but they're concerned. Do you suppose we could pray for her?"

That was like saying, "Sic 'em," to a hound dog.

Betty could sit in for her sister, and Betty's husband and I could follow Jesus' directives as outlined in Mark 16:17, 18: ". . . These signs shall follow them that believe. . . . In my name," Jesus said, ". . . they shall lay hands on the sick and they shall recover."

We had learned from other cases that the treatment worked by proxy, too, and so we were ready to pray with all boldness.

The enemy came along as usual, at this point, and put in his bid. "But suppose nothing happens? Then you'll look like fools."

"Who's looking?" we answered him. "Besides, we have the

155

word of God that this thing is worth doing. If nothing happens, well then we'll know we did it on our own, but if something happens, we'll give the glory to Jesus."

Slue Foot must have taken off at that, because we didn't hear anything further from him that trip.

Betty's husband and I laid hands on her, and prayed in the Spirit in a heavenly language we didn't understand. How else could I pray for someone I'd never met, someone I knew nothing about except that she had a serious ailment? In Romans 8:26 the Bible acknowledges that when we don't know how to pray, the Holy Ghost, who sees our infirmities, prays for us with words which are too deep for utterance. As we prayed, we could feel the power of the Holy Spirit backing us up.

Now I don't know what happened that day as a result of our prayers. I may not find out this side of heaven. But I know that something happened—because King's kids got together in obedience to the word of God. And I was glad a messed-up plane ticket let me be in on it. If I'd caught the right plane, the one that wasn't flying, I'd have missed all the glory time.

All things work together for good except a travel agent who doesn't keep up with schedule changes? Oh, no. God works his goofs together for good, too, as long as we love Him.

Have you ever worked yourself up into a nervous condition when somebody didn't treat you with the perfection you deserved? Now's the time to break up the pity-party, stop griping, and start praising God. Once you've done that, maybe events will shape up to make you glad things didn't go the way you had planned them.

Over the Frustration of Fouled-Up Flight Plans

Lord Jesus, I thank You that so often what looks like trouble is raw material for Your glory when we are obedient to trust You and praise You for it.

Forgive me that I've done so much griping, complaining, and murmuring against Your servants. I know now that's the same as murmuring against Your plans for my life. Cleanse me completely of this tendency, Lord, and set me to praising You continually so that You can use me for Your glory, too. In Jesus' name I ask it. Amen.

22

How to Be a Winner over No Room to Expand and No Money in the Bank

Pray without ceasing. (I Thessalonians 5:17)

Once upon a time, we needed expansion room in the Baptist church I was attending. We'd have moved some of our Sunday school classes to the basement, but the basement wasn't good for anything but a swimming pool when it rained, so we had to look elsewhere for additional meeting room. The ideal spot was right behind the church building. There were a couple of cottages there, just right for the Sunday morning overflow. But when our board of deacons approached the owner of the property, he shook his head.

"I will never sell those houses," he said, "especially to church people. And don't ask me to rent them out to you. I won't do that, either. As a matter of fact, for Baptists, I won't do anything."

The man hated Baptists—dead or alive, hard-boiled or fried. I never found out why, but I didn't have to know his motivation or understand anything about the situation. I knew God, and that was enough. He knew we needed space for our Sunday school program. And God is able to supply all our needs.

Three of us kooky charismaniacs went to the board of deacons and brought up an idea we had gotten out of the Bible. We wanted to pray for God to make the space available to us.

"Oh, we've prayed already," the deacons assured us. "On Sunday morning two months ago we made our requests known unto God." Nobody was surprised that nothing had happened. And they had already given it up as a hopeless cause.

God specializes in doing the impossible.

"But it says here that we're supposed to pray without ceasing," we said, pointing to I Thessalonians 5:17. "We've all prayed a little bit about this critical space situation, but how about if we started praying without ceasing, like maybe a chain of prayer around the clock at the altar of the church?"

The deacons were horrified. A little bit of prayer was okay according to their doctrine, but around the clock? That would be overdoing it, they thought.

We weren't surprised that they turned us down. If your attention is on failure, you'll fail. It's guaranteed. But if your attention is on God's promises—and ours was—there's no way you can do anything but succeed. We knew God's will was that we prosper and be in health as our souls prospered, and we knew, too, that whatever we did would prosper if we were faithful to keep sloshing around in the Word of God day and night. We'd gotten those insights from III John 2 and from the first Psalm. We were ready to test them out. It was God's word—it was supposed to work.

After the deacons turned us down, we went to see our pastor.

"Pastor, would it be all right with you if we tried something a little different in the church? Could we start a prayer chain on seven o'clock Saturday morning and go right around the clock until Sunday morning at seven? We wouldn't interfere with any meetings, and we'd be out before the Sunday school crowd came in—"

While he was thinking about it, we were praising God that tithing covers a multitude of charismatic manifestations. Because we were all tithers, the preacher wasn't interested in throwing us out. He checked the rules and found there were none to prohibit round-the-clock prayer in the church, so he didn't say no.

"But you'll never get folks interested in taking part, Brother Hill," he told me. "No one's going to get out of bed in the middle of the night to come down to the church and pray."

"Then it's okay if we try it?"

He okayed the program. Likely he figured it couldn't do any harm. He certainly didn't expect it to do any good. We did, though.

We got a big piece of posterboard, ruled it off in twenty-four hour intervals, and hung it on the church door.

"Sign up for whatever part of the twenty-four hours you can cover," we announced to the congregation.

The first weekend, people stayed away in droves. Only six people signed up. That meant each of us got to spend four hours at the altar on the average. Since some couldn't stay that long, others stayed longer. We were determined to have somebody praying and praising God around the clock. We had to find out if God's word was good advice for King's kids or if it was for the birds.

By the second weekend, there were eight people signed up. By the third, a whole dozen. And then it began to catch on with full force. People were lined up waiting for their turn.

●

Born losers throw pity-parties and get thrown as a result.
King's kid winners start prayer chains and get their hearts' desires.

●

With somebody at the altar around the clock, we could begin to feel power coming into that whole situation, and by the end of six weeks, the church had changed from a mood of hopeless discouragement to one of joyful anticipation.

The outward situation hadn't changed We still had a wet basement, a big mortgage, a leaky roof, and no place to expand. But we had God on our side, and we knew it, because we had gone over to His side in praise and prayer without ceasing. We had created an atmosphere for increase, for the crop to come forth.

It had to happen, or the rocks would have started exploding. Jesus said that if the people didn't shout their hosannas, the rocks would do it for them. I don't want to drive along the highway and hear a bunch of rocks saying, "There goes Brother Hill. He won't praise the Lord, so we have to do it for him."

I want to do my own praising, the rocks can do theirs, and even the trees will clap their hands. I want to pray without ceasing as long as I have breath to do it.

In less than three months after we had started praising God and praying around the clock about our building situation, the owner of the houses was outside the church after a Sunday morning service. He didn't waste time on preliminaries. He came right to the point.

"Some time ago you folks approached me about buying my property. Are you still interested?"

"We are."

"I'll let you have the houses for less than I could get on the market." He sounded quite disgusted with himself for making the offer. "I don't know why I'm doing this," he said, "because I didn't intend to sell to anybody, certainly not to a bunch of Baptists."

He said the word as if it was a bad taste in his mouth, and we were careful to keep our hallelujahs quiet.

"Come to my office tomorrow morning, and we'll close the deal," he said. "How much can you bring for a down payment?"

"We don't exactly have anything at this point," we told him. "We have a big debt, a plant that needs repair, and that's all. Can't get any more credit."

His eyes looked puzzled, as if the problem was his to solve and not ours. That was fine. If he would do the worrying about the down payment for us, we wouldn't have to.

163

"Tell you what I'll do," he said after a moment. "I'll take a second mortgage on the property and give you the cash to put down to make the whole thing legal. Will that be satisfactory?"

For a guy who hadn't intended to sell at all, he had made a real about-face.

"Sure," we said, "that will be all right," almost as if we were doing him a favor. And then we said something else. "We'll be able to give you back the down payment in sixty days."

I don't know where we came up with the sixty days' business. The down payment was $2500 and we didn't have twenty-five cents. Besides that, the bank was pushing us to pay them interest that we had owed them for more than two years on *our* mortgage.

"Well, Jesus," some of us prayed, "we thank You for getting the property for us. We don't know where You're going to get the $2500, but we're going to keep on praising You that that's Your business and not ours. If You could get that man to sell us the property when he didn't want to, and when we didn't have any money, we're sure You can handle this, too."

Actually, we knew God already had the money stashed away somewhere. King's kids have a wealthy Father. He owns all the cattle on a thousand hills, and all the hills under the cattle. Twenty-five hundred dollars would be a cinch for a landowner like that.

We kept up our prayer chain.

The next week, we had a visitor in our worship service, a stranger to our congregation. After the final hymn, he introduced himself to our pastor.

164

"I'm Brother so-and-so from the home mission board. I understand you folks are increasing the size of your plant here. As an expanding Baptist mission church, you're entitled to our donation of $2500." Nobody had asked for it, but the check was in the mail the next day.

With all the new space available for Sunday school, the neighborhood kids began to flock in. Our prayer chain kept going, and soon we needed to build an educational building. Practically everyone in the church got on the prayer chain for that. We were all wondering where God was going to get the money for such an expensive project. We certainly didn't have it, but God had it banked right in our own front yard. We found it out when the officials of Baltimore County came to see our board of deacons.

"We're going to widen the boulevard in front of your church," they said. "And we need a ten foot strip off the front of your property. You can sell it to us—or we can initiate condemnation proceedings."

King's kids always go willingly, so we told them our situation.

"That property is not ours," we said. "It belongs to our heavenly Father, so you'd better not condemn it."

They gave us a big fat check for more than enough to begin our $110,000 education building.

Things went from glory to glory for that church. It was on fire for Jesus until common sense and pride set in. Suddenly God's church became *our* "magnificent plant." It sounded as if they were talking about a tandem rolling mill.

Unteachableness and stiffness of neck that refused to move in any affirmative direction set in. That kind of deadly theology is guaranteed to kill everything around it. The inertia of the human mind can bring the best avalanche of blessing to a screeching halt. And it did.

"We're so prosperous, we don't need to ask the Lord for anything else," they said. "We already have a new organ in place of our old beat-up piano, so we can easily handle our future financial needs through our plan of finance. We don't need to bother God."

Their plan of finance was pretty good, but we had been operating under something much more beneficial. Still, the bulk of the people were of one accord, and do-it-myself-ism set in in epidemic proportions.

It was plain that the kooky charismatics were not needed any longer, so most of them moved out. I could almost hear Jesus weeping, *Oh, My children, I had everything for you, but you would not.*

Today, that church is struggling to stay alive because it stopped looking to the Lord to supply all its needs and began looking to itself. That always leads to second best, and in cases where there are only two choices, second best turns out to be the worst thing imaginable. In some situations, the difference between God's best and our own second best is the same as the difference between heaven and hell. Prosperity that lasts doesn't lie in self-sufficiency, but in looking to God for all things, praising Him continually and praying without ceasing.

Is there something you need? You don't have to win friends and influence people to get it. You just need to start a prayer chain and keep on praising God.

Father, I can see now that there's never any failure when I trust You, and I know that there's never been anything good about the world's ways compared to Your ways. Success in the world is nothing compared to success in You.

Lord, forgive me that for most of my life I've used the ways of the world to try to get what I wanted. I repent of all that right now. Let me turn all my impossibles over to You. Show me how to praise You for everything, to pray without ceasing, to give You all the glory and honor for supplying all my needs. I ask these blessings of being wholly dependent on You in Jesus' name. Amen.

23

How to Be a Winner
over People Who Steal

In everything give thanks: for this is the will of God in Christ Jesus concerning you. (I Thessalonians 5:18)

We were using a brand-new set of sound equipment at a CFO camp in North Carolina a few summers ago. Microphones, amplifiers, taping equipment—the whole works was fresh off the shelf. It was working beautifully, as it should have been. The outfit had cost a cool $3000 through a discount operation. We were all impressed with its excellence.

And then one morning, we were impressed with its absence. We arrived at the auditorium and discovered the back door open. Someone had broken in and stolen the whole business. The sound equipment had vanished without a trace.

We reported the theft to the police immediately, of

course, to the insurance company, and to the manager of the hotel where we were meeting.

"This kind of thing is happening all the time," the police chief told us. "There's a bunch of dope addicts around here, and they steal everything that isn't nailed down, to support their habits. I'm afraid you've seen the last of your equipment. You're lucky it was insured."

He shook his head and shoved our report into a drawer full of other reports of missing property. I figured the police weren't even going to try to find it for us because they felt it was a hopeless case.

Well, they were entitled to their opinion, based on their experience, but we had another kind of experience, an ace in the hole that the law enforcement agency hadn't heard about. Our experience had been that if we would trust God and thank Him for everything, we wouldn't have to settle for what invariably happens to people who aren't in on Kingdom living. King's kids don't know anything about failure. Considering God is for winners; considering failure is for losers.

> Everything in this world
> is good enough for its citizens,
> but not good enough for King's kids.

The CFO Council Ring got together and agreed that the equipment didn't belong to them to start with. It belonged to God Almighty. It was His equipment for spreading His word. And we agreed that He was certainly able to protect His own property. He already knew who the thieves were. He had been watching them the whole time they unplugged the stuff, and He knew where they were now and where they had cached the loot. All we had to do was to thank Him and see how He was going to work the whole thing together for good.

While we were thanking God that He could take care of the sound equipment, wherever it was, and praising Him for being Lord of all circumstances, the phone rang. Somebody wanted to speak to the guy in charge of the CFO meeting. A young boy was on the line.

•

Born losers stay poor carrying lots of insurance.
King's kid winners thank God for thieves and get their property returned as good as new.

•

"I guess you know by now that somebody broke in last night and walked off with your sound equipment," he said.

"Yeah," the CFO man acknowledged. "We kind of found that out when we looked for the microphone this morning."

"Well, I'm one of the guys who took it, but we've changed our minds about selling it to get some money," the boy said. "We'd like to give it back to you."

The CFO man kind of leaned against the wall to hold himself up. He had expected God to act, but not quite that fast. His voice almost left him, but he managed to get out two pertinent questions: "When?" and "Where?"

"I can't tell you where it is just yet," the boy said, "because the police are after us. We're addicts and we needed the money for dope. I'll call back at six tonight to tell you where to pick up your equipment." The receiver clicked and the voice was gone.

Well, we had something good to thank the Lord for now.

171

Our stuff that was lost had been found. And surely it was God who had changed the boys' minds and made them decide to contact us. That meant He was working in their lives, too. We were on shouting ground, having a glory fit right then and there.

The hotel manager kept shaking his head. He thought we were more than unusually gullible.

"They'll never call back," he said. "Too risky. Your stuff is gone for good."

"Forget it," the police chief agreed. "They're just playing games with you. They don't ever give back what they've stolen."

We just kept on thanking God for taking care of His property so well, and we thanked Him for speaking to the boys.

At six o'clock the phone rang again.

"Look under some empty packing cases behind the Howard Johnson's restaurant," a boy's voice said. "Goodbye." Click.

"You're just wasting your time," the hotel manager and police chief said when we piled into a truck to go get God's equipment.

"We're quite willing to do that," we told them between hallelujahs, and headed for the restaurant.

There it was, just as the boy had said. Perfect condition, everything intact, all ready for setting up for the night meeting.

Panic? Not for King's kids. Praising and thanking is what they do best. And they do it all the time. God hears and turns the bad things into good things for His kids.

All the nerves of our spiritual bodies are on the outside

when we're standing up for our own rights and protecting our own property. That's a pretty tender situation. No wonder we get hurt so bad. It's as if we're turned inside out, with no callouses to protect our insides on the outside. Everything that touches you hurts like crazy when you're protecting your own rights. And everything that touches you blesses you when you're in the high gear of praise, when you look to God with thanksgiving and ask, "Lord, what's in this for You?"

In the high gear of praising and thanking God, you're turned right side out. That's wrong side out according to the ways of the world, of course. The world says you should stand up for your rights, protect your property, and get mad whenever your rights are infringed upon. But God says that if you belong to Him, you don't have any rights to stand up for, and you don't own any property to protect. It all belongs to Him.

When adversity comes, the natural reaction of most people is to panic or to blame something on somebody. But King's kids praise and give thanks instead. And they live in victory no matter what happens.

How are things in your own life? Have you been feeling sorry for yourself because someone took something that had your name on it or because someone moved in to a place you thought was reserved for you? Are you tired of living in misery because the world has abused you by taking away your rights or your property?

Are you ready to be set free to act instead of to react? Are you ready to turn the management of all your affairs over to the One who made you to walk in victory?

If you are, then you can pray your own prayer to give the good news to your Maker, or you can try this one for size. Whichever one you pray, God will hear and answer.

Lord Jesus, I'm sorry that I've been so dense, hanging onto my misery so tightly when You wanted to give me a life that was abundant. Forgive me that I've been fearful instead of rejoicing. Just enter into me today in such a way that I'll be set free to praise You continually, to marvel at what You're doing for me now that I'm taking my hands off things and letting You have free rein.

And Lord, help me to forgive all those who have ever taken anything from me. Bless them, Lord, and save them out of their misery, too. Hallelujah! Thank You, Lord, for making me a part of the answer instead of a part of the problem. In Jesus' name. Amen.

24

How to Be a Winner
over Deceiving Spirits

Enter ye in at the strait gate; for wide is the gate, and broad is the way, that leadeth to destruction and many there be which go in thereat: Because strait is the gate, and narrow is the way which leadeth unto life, and few there be that find it.

Beware of false prophets, which come to you in sheep's clothing, but inwardly they are ravening wolves. Ye shall know them by their fruits. (Matthew 7:13-16)

One day I received a note in the mail from a certain Mr. Microbe of Baltimore.

"We understand you have had some experience with healing in prayer groups," he wrote. "We know nothing about prayer, but we have had some experiences in treating people for illness, too. If you would like to come and share your prayer group experience with us, we'll share with you what we have found."

Well, that sounded like a fascinating evening, so I telephoned the man, and we set a date.

When I arrived on the appointed evening, Mr. Microbe, who said he was a psychologist, took me back to his laboratory in a rear bedroom of his home. It was all set up with tape recorders, medical files, case histories, and very meticulously kept records. Mr. Microbe introduced me to another man—I'll call him Mr. Virus—who acted as a medium for the "healing" session.

"You are the first outsider we have ever invited to observe these things, Mr. Hill," Mr. Microbe told me. "We'll show you how we work, and we'll be glad to hear your reactions afterward as well as your own experience with prayer."

I nodded my understanding, and the session began.

•

Born losers try to be broad-minded and wind up in devilish deception that leads to the funny farm.
King's kid winners choose the straight and narrow path that leads to eternal life in the heavenlies and in the here and now.

•

When Mr. Virus stretched out on the bed and went into a trance-like state, I recognized immediately that I was in the midst of a bunch of Edgar Cayce-ites.

"Lord," I prayed, "cover me with Your blood in this situation. I thank You that You are powerful enough to protect me from the deception that surrounds me."

How did I know it was deception? From personal experience. I'd gone the Edgar Cayce route myself back in my pagan days.

"Let me see a miracle of Your power here tonight, Lord," I went on. "Let me see a miracle that will expose Satan for what he is—a liar and a cheat." I knew that when God is in charge, there are no goof-ups, but Satan can't avoid goofing—it's programmed into his computer.

Having prayed in silence with my understanding, I proceeded to pray in the Spirit. In the name of Jesus, victory was sure to come.

When Mr. Virus intoned, "I'm ready," Mr. Microbe said, "Case history number one. Mr. so-and-so. How are conditions?"

A muffled voice, which sounded as if it was coming from down deep inside a moldy cave, spoke through Mr. Virus, saying, "Some improvement. Continue with prescribed treatment."

It was all very impressive. If I hadn't been aware of what was going on, keeping myself on God's wavelength by praying in the Spirit, I might have been deceived into thinking all this was great stuff.

Mr Microbe made a check mark on a card and put it back into the file. He continued to call out case numbers and patient names. Mr. Virus continued to intone muffled words as to the nature of the improvement and the recommended treatment. At case history number twelve, a patient by the name of Mrs. Muddled, something electric alerted me to take very careful notice.

"Mr. Virus, how is Mrs. Muddled's asthma?"

The muffled voice came back, "No change. Same as before."

Suddenly, in the Spirit, I saw an x-ray picture of the inside of Mrs. Muddled! The gift of discernment and the word of knowledge—two gifts of the Spirit working together—had given me information no one had up to that point. I was so excited, I almost blurted out, "Hey! You goofed on that one." But God checked me. He seemed to say, *Wait. I'll let you know when to uncork this one.*

I managed to restrain myself while they went methodically through some more case records. At the end, Mr. Virus returned from the spook dimension and sat up on the bed.

"What's your reaction?" the Messrs. Microbe and Virus wanted to know. They obviously expected me to be overwhelmed.

I shrugged.

"Well, I'm quite familiar with Edgar Cayce methods," I told them. "But I got free of all that years ago. Actually, you did pretty well, all things considered. But in the case of Mrs. Muddled, you really blew it."

"What do you mean, we blew it? Are you psychic or something?"

"Oh, no. Not psychic. That's for the birds. I'm saved and filled with God's Holy Spirit. That means I'm hooked up to the Head Man of the universe. Jesus is His name. And by the gift of discerning of spirits, He showed me what's wrong with Mrs. Muddled. It's not what you're treating her for. No wonder she's not getting well."

"Impossible!" Virus shouted.

"It can't be!" Microbe agreed.

But it was. They listened while I told them, "Mrs. Muddled doesn't have asthma, she has emphysema. I saw the leathery condition inside her lungs. If you'll get out your records, you'll probably see where you made your mistake."

"I believe you're right," Mr. Microbe acknowledged after looking through all the charts in the woman's file. "We made a wrong diagnosis. We've been treating Mrs. Muddled for the wrong thing."

No arrangement of bad eggs
makes a good omelet.

I let the matter rest. Then I told them how I had been involved in Edgar Cayce and all the other cults once upon a time, but I'd since met Jesus, the real thing, and gotten rid of all the counterfeits.

"There's no chance of goofing when God's in charge," I told them. "He lets us read it straight and clear, because He's the only one who has all knowledge."

Part of my testimony had to do with how Jesus set me free from nicotine in the days when I was a constant chimney. When Jesus set me free, He did a thorough job. I didn't even have to substitute a mint or chewing gum. My habit was gone, clean gone. I noticed that Mr. Microbe was really listening to all that while he puffed on one coffin nail after another, coughing like he was about to lose his insides. When I went home, I had a feeling I would be invited back. There was unfinished business in that house.

The following week, Mr. Microbe telephoned me.

"I have a problem, Mr. Hill," he began. "I cannot quit smoking. It's killing me, destroying my lungs. The doctors have warned me that I have to quit or else. But I've tried, and I can't. Now, the other night you told us how you had quit—"

"Hold it!" I interrupted. "I told you no such thing. What I said was that I had tried, and I found that I couldn't quit either. The harder I tried, the worse I got. But Jesus took my nicotine addiction away from me."

He was in no mood for quibbling.

"Well, anyhow, you don't smoke any more, right?"

"That's right."

"So would you come over and pray for me so I can be rid of the nicotine, too?"

"Gladly."

Knowing this was not an assignment for one man, I telephoned my prayer buddy.

"Get your praying britches on, Ed. We've got a hot one tonight—right in Slue Foot's home camp."

It's a good idea to travel in pairs when you deal with spooks. One can pray while the other witnesses. Jesus sent them out by twos for a purpose. There is ten times the power when two King's kids are together, agreeing with one another and with God. If I had been alone that night, I might have gotten into real trouble.

"Don't stop praying, no matter what," I told Ed, "or we will be in bad shape." I knew that Satan couldn't come into the circle of light that surrounds King's kids when they keep on praying in the Spirit. Darkness is swallowed up when it is invaded by light. It doesn't work the other way around in the world of physics or in the spiritual realm. Light is always the overcomer. Since darkness is a nothingness, an absence of energy, it doesn't have any power to fight with.

When Ed and I arrived at Mr. Microbe's house, the lights

were all turned low. We found Mr. Microbe apparently alone in the house, but I could feel eyeballs staring at us from all over the place. Satan's power was present with suffocating darkness. I was glad Ed and I were prayed up so that the power of evil couldn't touch us. I felt as I'd felt in places of demon worship in the West Indies where voodoo practitioners make dolls and stick pins in them. In a few weeks, the person represented by the doll can be good and dead unless he's wearing the full armor of God. We had ours on full strength.

The helmet of salvation was the blood of Jesus to ward off the attacks on our minds so we wouldn't be deceived. The breastplate of righteousness was Jesus Himself, protecting our vital organs from invasion by the enemy. Jesus is the only righteousness we'll ever have. Our feet were shod with the preparation of the gospel. And we had the shield of faith and the sword of the Spirit, which is the word of God.

Mr. Microbe invited us into the laboratory in the back bedroom again. There Ed kept praying a backup prayer while I talked to Mr. Microbe.

"As I told you on the telephone," Mr. Microbe began, getting right down to business, "I'm in terrible shape physically from smoking. I'd like for you to pray for me."

"Fine. That's what we came for. But before we pray, there's something you need to understand. We ourselves have nothing to offer, but we rely on the One who has all power. His name is Jesus, and we will pray in His name, if that is satisfactory. That name contains all power in heaven and on earth."

As we reached toward Mr. Microbe to lay our hands on him, he leaped out of his chair.

"That is totally *un*satisfactory!" he shouted.

Satan was beginning to show his slimy hand. Up till that time, Mr. Microbe had pretended to be a Christian. But suddenly, Satan was in full charge of him.

"Unsatisfactory? I don't understand. What's wrong with it?" I asked him.

"Jesus is an impostor!"

"Is He really? Who told you?" At this point, my questions weren't coming out of my own intellect, and I knew it.

"Our friends, the good spirits. They're the ones who told us that Jesus is a curse, a nasty name, an impostor." Mr. Microbe was highly agitated. He almost came out of his skin. Ed and I, on the other hand, were resting in Jesus in an almost supernatural calm.

The questions continued to come through me.

"Does your god have a name, Mr. Microbe?"

"Yes. His name is Tyrus."

Tyrus! What a revelation! The island of Tyre was so demon-ridden, that God had destroyed it. The wicked Jezebel had come from Tyre.

I wanted nothing further to do with Mr. Microbe as long as he was part of that outfit. Ed and I turned to leave.

"Is your god all powerful?" I asked Mr. Microbe as we were going out of the room.

"Of course," he coughed.

"Well, then, why don't you ask your powerful god Tyrus to get you off cigarettes?" I said over my shoulder. "Meanwhile, while you're coughing yourself to death, we'll be on our way. When you're ready for us to pray in the name of Jesus, call us. We'll be glad to come back."

Mr. Microbe's face was contorted with a demonic snarl of

fury, but the power of the name of Jesus kept him from attacking us. As Ed and I walked through the living room toward the outside door, praying without ceasing down in our gizzards, I saw a circle of demons squatting around the walls of the room—little gnomes, with swelled heads and shrunken bodies, turtle faces, frog physiognomies, devils straight from the pit.

I praised God for the ring of fire I could feel around my head. It warded off the evil spirits and kept them at their distance. When Ed and I had reached the sidewalk, I looked at him. His bald head was pure lily white. I didn't feel too pink myself. But we had a new testimony of how the blood of Jesus could protect from evil.

Satan's tricks are all around us these days. We'll fall for them if we don't watch out, if we don't keep ourselves prayed up and tuned into God's circuit of heavenly joy and peace.

False teachings and doctrines of devils are creeping in everywhere, even into churches, conferences, and retreats. Many who call themselves Christians are being drawn into the abominations of the occult—Edgar Cayce, witchcraft, horoscopes, transcendental meditation, mind control, and Ouija boards, to name just a few. Any Christian who falls into these things becomes a retarded Christian. He chooses to believe a lie instead of the truth of God.

Maybe you thought that Edgar Cayce was a good guy, and that his followers were good guys, too. Think again. Satan is never a good guy, even when he comes disguised as an angel of light. The fact that healings take place does not prove a thing is of God. Anything of God exalts Jesus. The Edgar Cayce-ites do not exalt Jesus. Physical healing of the body is second-best compared to the wholeness that Jesus delivers. Healing is merely two-dimensional; wholeness is three-dimensional, a package deal.

Satan's counterfeit might look like the real thing, but it only patches up an old garment. Jesus delivers brand-new merchandise—wholeness. Tuned-in and turned-on King's kids can tell the difference. They go first class.

"But I don't see anything wrong with reading my horoscope or playing with a Ouija board," some of you may argue. "After all, it's all in fun. Just a game. I don't really live by it."

If you're one who feels that way, Satan has you right where he wants to keep you. God calls these things abominations because they invariably draw His people further and further from Him and eventually suck them all the way into the camp of the enemy.

Don't be a loser by following the reasonable dictates of your think tank. That could lead you to permanent residency as an inmate on the funny farm, because "the whole head is sick (Isaiah 1:5). Follow Jesus instead, all the way to abundant and eternal life.

A Spirit-filled Christian can recognize which wavelengths are of God and which are not of Him. The retarded Christian will try to guess what's going on, and Slue Foot will sneak up on his blind side and draw him into deception. He will choose to believe a lie instead of the truth. It takes all the gifts of the Spirit for King's kids to function victoriously in these days.

Operating with the gifts of the Spirit is not supposed to be spectacular, out of the ordinary. It's normal Christian living when you're walking in the Spirit. Heal the sick. Cast out devils. Take care of needs by the power of the Holy Spirit working through you.

Over Deceiving Spirits

I imagine Mr. Microbe is still coughing his insides out. When he gets up to ten packs a day, he may be ready to let us pray for him in the name of Jesus. While his false god Tyrus is doing nothing for him, the testimony of kooky Christians will keep nagging at him until he's won over. That's how it works. Walk into the midst of trouble, and announce, "I have the answer. The answer is Jesus. If you want Him, you can have deliverance. If you don't want Him, forget it and get worse."

It sounds cruel, but you're actually doing the person a favor. They need to know that Jesus is the only One who can help them. Put them on your icky prayer list. Pray that they go from one degree of misery to another until they receive Him.

Think you're not worthy to have anything happen when you give your testimony or when you pray for someone? Satan is always around to tell you you're not worthy to do what God calls you to do. I don't argue with him. I agree with him one hundred per cent.

"You're right, Slue Foot, I'm not worthy. I'll never be," I tell him.

"You don't have what it takes," he tells me next.

"I certainly don't," I agree.

"You're going to blow this one completely."

"Right on," I tell him. "If I'm in charge, I'll ruin everything. But Jesus happens to be in charge of my life and my functioning, and therefore Romans 8:1 applies to me: 'There is therefore now no condemnation to them which are in Christ Jesus, who walk not after the flesh but after the Spirit.' " Satan doesn't stick around to hear the end of the verse, because he knows I have him licked this time.

Satan will always say you're condemned. But God says you're not. Which one will you believe?

Anytime you feel condemned, that heaviness, that burdened feeling, is coming from Slue Foot. In Canada, they call him Old Dirty Face, the accuser of the brethren. Whatever you call him, know that he wants to make you think that God can't use you. He doesn't want God to use anybody. But you don't have to let him have his way. You can let God have His way in you.

Never think negatively about what God can do through you. When the power of God is in you to make it happen, and you're tuned up to the power circuit where Jesus can make it happen, it will happen.

Ten or twelve years ago, I took part in a Faith at Work weekend conference up in Ontario. A young boy there met Jesus in a marvelous way—as Baptizer in the Holy Spirit. Afterward, he went home to the farmhouse where his twelve brothers and sisters lived with him and his parents. They all listened to his testimony. He told them how he had met Jesus, and how his life was different already. He couldn't put it all into words, but when he said, "Jesus is so real to me," they believed him. He looked different, he sounded different. They couldn't understand it, but they said, "Whatever it is that you got, we need it, too."

The whole family got down on their knees together and praised God. As they prayed, all fourteen—the twelve brothers and sisters and the boy's parents—were filled with the Holy Spirit.

That started something among the young people in Ontario. Many began carrying their Bibles with them.

"What are you, a bunch of kooks?" their friends would ask them.

"Yes, we're kooks for Jesus," the turned-on young people said, and by the word of their testimony, God began to change the whole province.

Jesus takes us with whatever equipment we have or do not have and provides the entire wherewithal to do what He wants to do through us. All we have to do is believe that He can.

Go into action wherever you know God wants the good news to be spread. Spirit is energy, and it takes action for energy to become power. The kingdom of God is the energy of righteousness, peace, and joy in the Holy Ghost. When you get the body moving and put it into action, then the kingdom of God is power in evidence to break down the kingdom of darkness and to bring into evidence the kingdom of our God. Hallelujah!

If you've been deceived by anything not of God, you can confess it now and be rid of it forever. Cleansed by the forgiving blood of Jesus, you can begin to walk in newness of life, being a winner, living like a King's kid instead of a Shantytown brat who has to settle for second best. And you can make a difference by the word of your testimony

Thank You, Lord Jesus, that You haven't wiped me out for dabbling in the things that are abominations to You. I confess all my sins in this realm: (NAME THE WEIRD THINGS THAT HAVE HAD YOUR ATTENTION. READ DEUTERONOMY 18:9-12 FOR A LIST OF SOME OF THEM TO REFRESH YOUR MEMORY).

Forgive me for being fascinated by Edgar Cayce when You can do so much better. Forgive me for reading horoscopes to determine how I should conduct my life instead of seeking to know Your plan for it. Forgive me for looking to seances and witchcraft and mind control and reincarnation and psychics for answers that belong to You alone. Forgive me for thinking that Ouija boards were just innocent fun. Forgive me for not giving Your word at least equal time with the boob tube.

Forgive me, Lord, for settling for second best in any area of my life. Let me live the life You have planned for me from now on. Let me never again seek truth from any source that does not give You the full glory.

Lord, thank You that even though I've fallen for deception in the past, even though I've royally goofed so many areas of my life, You still love me. Thank You for keeping me from getting into even worse trouble. Help me to use the power of discernment You have given me so that I won't get drawn into anything else that is not of You. Thank You for opening my eyes and for making me aware of my sin. Thank You for revealing the lie of Satan's tricks, for the gift of discernment from the Holy Spirit to show what he's up to.

Thank You, Lord, for Your power that protects me from evil. Thank You for Your forgiving love. Thank You for the power of our testimony of Your grace. And thank You for giving me Your mind, the mind of a winner over all circumstances, in place of my natural mind, that of a born loser. Thank You, Lord, for letting me be born again. In Jesus' name. Amen.

25

How to Be a Winner over Heart Attacks and Other Intensive-care Ailments

. . . My grace is sufficient for thee: for my strength is made perfect in weakness. (II Corinthians 12:9)

Has Jesus really overcome the final enemy, death itself? He said He had, and I'd believed it. Sometimes I'd even quoted the Scripture, "Death is swallowed up in victory. . . . Thanks be to God, which giveth the victory through our Lord Jesus Christ" (I Corinthians 15:54, 57). But it's one thing to believe something and another thing to *know* it. Today I *know* that Jesus has swallowed up death in victory, because I personally checked that Scripture out in September of 1975.

From about midnight until two o'clock in the morning that September night, I was lying in my bed at home praising the Lord with increasing difficulty. The feeling over my heart was as if a piano leg—concert grand, with six grossly over-weight people perched on top of it—was resting on me. As a result, I couldn't rest. It was a highly interesting sensation, but not one I wanted to enjoy indefinitely, even with praises coming from my lips.

I woke my wife and managed to stammer, "You'd-better-get-me-some-help."

Our daughter, being a medical secretary, knew just who to call and how to get things into action without delay. I was wheeled into the emergency room of the hospital within less than forty minutes. By that time, I had no business being anywhere else. I was an emergency all right. Things were super-critical. It was my second heart attack within a week.

An old friend just happened to be the emergency doctor on duty that night. He started using his stethoscope while a nurse wound my arm up for a blood pressure reading.

> The soul always looks at symptoms,
> and faints at the dire diagnosis.
> The Spirit rejoices,
> seeing a perfect prognosis in Jesus.

"Fifty over zero," I heard her report just before blackness set in. My pastor had arrived, and I heard him praising God. My daughter was saying, "Thank You, Jesus," and that's all I remember for a while.

When I came back to this world, I was aware that I had not been afraid during my absence, and that I actually felt cheated out of graduation because the saints were praising God and interceding for me with perfect prayers. Maybe the quota for my particular type was temporarily filled up yonder. I don't know. But whatever the reason for my return, I had no anxiety about going—then or now. I was willing to be with Jesus at whatever level of earth or heaven He thought was best. It didn't matter to me which way He decided or why.

In the days that followed, as I lay in the intensive-care unit, I found myself asking just one question: "Lord, what's in this for You?" Being that close to death—and that was just one of four heart attacks within the month, as it turned out—cleanly stripped me of all anxieties and purposes of my own.

"Lord, You've got a reason for me to be back here in the cardiac intensive-care unit," I prayed. "Show me what it is."

•

Born losers try to stay strong in their own strength and get weaker and weaker from the wasted effort.
King's kid winners offer their weakness to God and He fills it up to overflowing with His strength.

•

He didn't give me any immediate answer, so I just waited. There wasn't much else I could do. I was all connected up to wires and pipes and tubes and hoses, so computerized, I couldn't wiggle my big toe without having some technician pop up at my side to see what was wrong.

The man in the bed beside mine had had the pronouncement of doom spoken over him. It was obvious that the hospital staff expected him to go out feet first, with his head under the sheet.

His doctor came in one morning and said, "Harry, you've been rushed into intensive-care eight times this year. Every test indicates that you are an alcoholic. You've ruined your liver. It's completely wrecked. One more drink, one more drop of alcohol, and it's curtains for you. As a matter of fact," he went on, "I'm not sure you're going to live this time."

After Harry's doctor went out, I turned to the patient and asked him, "What are you going to do after you get out of here?" Somehow I figured he would have one last chance to make it.

"Get some booze and pull a drunk. What else?" he answered.

"But I thought I heard the doctor say that you can't drink any more unless you want to climb in a casket."

"Oh," he said, "the doc exaggerates. He can't scare me. I'm not that bad off. Why, I'm not really an alcoholic even. I don't drink in the daytime."

"I wasn't that bad, either," I told him, suddenly aware of what I was doing in the intensive-care unit. You can't get in there for any length of time unless you're a paying customer or part of the medical contingent.

"I didn't drink in the daytime," I told Harry, "and I kept my job. But after a lot of years, I realized that alcohol was running my life and I was unable to do anything about it. I had become an alcoholic. It kind of sneaked up on me."

Harry did a double-take. Under sheets, it's hard to tell much about another patient.

"You're an alcoholic?" he said in disbelief.

"A non-practicing one, however," I assured him. "My alcoholism is my weakness, but it became my greatest strength when I turned it over to Jesus. He remade my life when I admitted I couldn't handle it any longer by myself."

Harry and I talked practically around the clock after that. In the cardiac unit, other opportunities for recreation were rather limited. I learned that Harry was a multimillionaire, a guy who had everything in the world to live for but yet nothing that counted.

Harry left the hospital on Thursday, carrying with him a copy of *How to Live Like a King's Kid* that my daughter had smuggled into the hospital. A few days later, Harry came back to visit me.

"The greatest trip I ever had was when I came to this hospital the last time," he said. "I just wanted to let you know that I've read your book, and I'm going to my first AA meeting tonight."

"Thank You, Jesus," I said. "My ICU stay was worth the trip. There *was* something in it for You—Harry."

Six months have passed as I write this. Harry hasn't had a drink since. He hasn't been in the intensive-care unit of a hospital again, either. He's being intensively cared for by Jesus, and is living it up like a real winner.

Do you have a weakness? Years ago, acutely aware of my weakness, I cried out, "God help me," and with that, I was on my way to glory land. Your weakness can be your greatest strength, too, as you let God's strength be manifested through it.

If you do have a weakness, and you've been trying to camouflage it, trying to cover it up and hide it even from God, don't do that any longer. Your weakness may be your greatest asset as you let God move into it and transform your life by His strength and power.

Can you praise God for your weakness and ask Him to use it to His glory?

Lord Jesus, I thank You that Your strength can be made manifest in my weakness. I thank You that I don't have to cover it up, to rationalize my behavior, and keep on disintegrating with the stresses and strains of it all. I'm glad I can come to You right now and say, "Lord, I thank You for my weakness." Thank You, Jesus, that You've allowed it to come to my attention. Thank You that I can turn it over to You that Your strength and power might be manifested in it. Thank You that I may show forth Your power to the world by the testimony of what You have done for me, that others may be made ready to receive You for themselves.

Lord, thank You for the paradox of it all, for the blessing of knowing You, for the weakness that made me turn in Your direction after all that time of misery.

Lord, I'm ready to let You lead me by the still waters and restore my soul from troublesome ownership for myself to troublefree stewardship for You. Thank You that You have made it so that my ownership can never make me anything more than a loser but that Your ownership makes me a winner—entitled to and receiving all of heaven's best.

Make use of me as You see fit, Lord. Help Yourself to me completely. And if I'm still not quite sure I want You to do that, do it anyhow. Thank You, Jesus. Amen.

I'm signing up and reporting in for experiencing more of the benefits of King's kid living. I'm ready to become a member of the winners' team by selling out to You completely, Jesus, as Lord of my life. That makes it Your life in me, and what You do with it is Your business.

_____
Name   Date

_____
Name   Date

_____
Name   Date

Other books by Harold Hill:
How to Live Like a King's Kid
From Goo to You by Way of the Zoo